He Loved Them to the End

*Theological Meditations
on Love and Eucharist*

by Bruno Forte

translated by

Robert D. Paolucci

St. Paul Books & Media

Nihil Obstat
     Rev. Paul E. Ritt, STD

Imprimatur
     + Bernard Cardinal Law
     January 5, 1993

Library of Congress Cataloging-in-Publication Data

Forte, Bruno.
     He loved them to the end : theological meditations / Bruno Forte :
translated by Robert D. Paolucci.
          p.   cm.
     Writings originally appearing in 2 previously published works:
Sull'amore, and Corpus Christi.
     ISBN 0-8198-3369-X
     1. God—Love. 2. Trinity. 3. Lord's Supper—Catholic Church.
4. Catholic Church—Doctrines. I. Title.
BT140.F67   1993
231'.6—dc20   93-2770
                                                                    CIP

Printed and published in the U.S.A. by St. Paul Books & Media,
50 St. Paul's Avenue, Boston, MA 02130.

St. Paul Books & Media is the publishing house of the Daughters of
St. Paul, an international congregation of women religious serving the
Church with the communications media.

                    1 2 3 4 5 6 7 8 9   99 98 97 96 95 94 93

Contents

Preface 5

PART ONE—LOVE

1. The Trinity as Love's
   Eternal Event 11
2. The Dialogue of Love 55

PART TWO—EUCHARIST

3. Eucharist and Communion 81
4. Eucharist and Mission 105

Prayer of Thanksgiving and Petition 119

Notes 123

Preface

"He loved them to the end" (John 13:1). With these words John introduces the washing of the feet and Jesus' farewell discourse (which corresponds to the Last Supper scene of the synoptics), as well as the Lord's passion and resurrection. Thus, the evangelist invites us to contemplate the supreme revelation of Love in the "hour of Jesus" and in the eucharistic memorial by which it is made present in our lives.

Entering into the passion narrative with loving intelligence, we become capable of recognizing the eternal Love of the Trinity, accomplished in the silence of the Cross and the light of Easter (chapter 1). This event of love lived to the end reveals the intimate communication that unites the Father, Son and Holy Spirit among themselves and with the world, as well as the possibility that we, too, can learn to love and to communicate in love (chapter 2).

The "hour of Jesus," in which he loved us to the end, is made present in the eucharistic memorial, for at the Lord's Supper we can contemplate the mystery of our oneness in him (chapter 3) and our consequent responsibility for service and mission (chapter 4).

Thus, these two ways of delving into the mystery proclaimed in "He loved them to the end," lead us to the contemplation of the Trinity and invite us to make our contemplation a nourishing and life-giving experience by means of the bread of life. The theological and spiritual journey proposed in this book manifests the trinitarian profundity of the affirmation of Kahlil Gibran's prophet: "When you love, you should not say: I have God in my heart, but rather you should say: I am in the heart of God."

This radiant truth responds to the most genuine and profound question that the human heart can ask: Where and how can I learn how to love?

> Bruno Forte
> Advent, 1992:
> on pilgrimage toward the celebration
> of God's perennially youthful Love

Part One

Love

Introduction

Theology is not sophisticated "love for wis-dom" reserved for the few people engaged in the field. It is primarily the "wisdom of love," the attempt to put into words for others the lived experience of love. It is the attempt to recount the *history* of love, revealed to us in the life of Jesus of Nazareth, Lord and Christ, so as to inspire daily histories of love among the humble people of the earth. We could say that theology is the "teach-ing of faith," insofar as it is the "teaching of love"—i.e., it attempts to put into words and to bring about anew that lived experience of love which God's Word, received in faith, produces in the lives of the humble.

Theology is "love seeking understanding." It is love that wants to be declared, so that by being declared it may influence the deeds and days of humankind. The theologian "speaks of God, re-counting the story of love" (F. Jüngel), in pro-found awareness that love's reality is always inexpressible and transcendent. However hard one tries to speak of love, as manifested and offered in the earthly life of him who loved us to the end and continues to love us: this love will always be greater than words.

Everything that a theologian, as theologian, says about love is only an introduction to the experience and deepening of love. It is by no means a full and final word. The word calls love forth, arouses it and humbly serves it, but the word cannot restrict love; love remains something greater. When we speak of love in the ordinary affairs of the present world, we know its mystery only in the dimness of the twilight hours. To know it in the clear light of day is reserved for another time, for another homeland. Theological words about love defer to the silence of a love that is lived, which best anticipates the fullness of that future day when God will be everything in everyone and the whole world will be the home of his love.

The reflections that follow bear witness to the humble and initial effort that a theologian must make to speak about love and help his brothers and sisters to love.

1. The Trinity as Love's Eternal Event

The Exile of the Trinity and the Pilgrimage to the Trinitarian Homeland

Although belief in the Trinity is rightly considered the "turning point of a steadfast or declining Christian faith," the Trinity seems to have been banished from Christian theory and practice. "We may venture to say that if the doctrine of the Trinity were to be suppressed as being false, a fairly good portion of religious literature would remain nearly unchanged in the aftermath....We may suspect that in the catechism of mind and heart, as contrasted with the printed catechism, the representation of the Incarnation by Christians would not undergo any change at all if there were no Trinity."[1]

This situation is also the consequence of a theology that was concerned with safeguarding the divine oneness in view of a "pious" preoccupation with the Jewish and Hellenistic worlds (fascinated by the mystery of the One Being). At times this preoccupation had fallen into a misguided essentialism, exalting the unity of the divine essence to the point of giving the impression that the Trinity was a superfluous heavenly theorem: "From the doctrine of the Trinity, taken literally, it is absolutely impossible to extract anything of practical value, even if we were to believe that we understand the Trinity, much less as we realize, of course, that it surpasses our every conception."[2]

And this is how different theological treatises dealt with creation and redemption, anthropology and Christology. There was little concern for dealing with these different aspects from the specific Christian standpoint of faith in the Trinitarian God and of the sacred account of his love offered to us.

Morality itself was developed without any connection with this mystery, as though Christian activity were not the unfolding in lived experience (the Amen of life!) of the profession of belief in the Trinity that opens and closes the actions of the faithful: "In the name of the Father and of the Son and of the Holy Spirit.... Glory to the Father and to the Son and to the Holy Spirit!"

This isolation of trinitarian doctrine from the rest of dogma and ethics has not been overcome, even in many of our present-day theologies.

Whether it is a matter of new formulations of old treatises or of innovative intuitions or explorations, from hermeneutics to narrative theology, from political theology to liberation theology, the "trinitarian gospel" does not seem to play a really decisive role. It is no exaggeration to say that we are still witnessing a banishment of the Trinity from Christian theory and practice. But perhaps it is this banishment that makes persons experience nostalgia and gives rise to a beautiful rediscovery of the "trinitarian homeland" in theology and in life.

To end the Trinity's exile from the thinking and practice of the faithful, a renewed marriage of the Trinity with history is needed, which can be brought about through a return to the sacred account of our Christian roots—the history of revelation. Such is the profound meaning of Karl Rahner's basic axiom: "The economic Trinity is the immanent Trinity."[3]

This means that for knowing and experiencing God there is no point of departure from which one can speak of the divine mystery less unfaithfully than the history of revelation—the intimately connected events and words through which God has narrated his own history within ours. (The Fathers of the Church called God's ordered plan his "economy": the "dispensation" of the gift from on high that saves us). The Trinity as it is in itself—"immanent"—is made known through the

Trinity as it is for us—"economic." The Father in himself is one and the same with the God who reveals himself: the Father through the Son in the Holy Spirit.

This correspondence is grounded in the very mystery of divine faithfulness. If the immanent Trinity did not correspond to its revelation in the divine economy, no salvation in history would be possible. The human would irrevocably be confined within human horizons, and no glimmer of hope would pierce the painful experience of our finite condition. Nothingness would engulf all. But if, instead, "the sunset of death cannot engulf the divine" (Arnobius) and this divine life is truly made accessible to us in the history of Jesus Christ, then we too have been given the hope of an undying and full life. In the correspondence between the economy and immanence of the mystery, the Trinity offers itself as the reality of salvation and the experience of grace!

If the economy of the mystery corresponds to its immanence, to think of God as Trinity in the light of revelation means "thinking of God from within God, and therefore fathoming the Christian concept of divinization.... The concept of the Triune God is wholeheartedly accepted by the person who believes also that he or she has been included in the Triune God by the saving act of the Incarnate Word and the divinizing Spirit."[4]

When we consider the Trinity without separating history from glory, we are thus considering ourselves. Our human condition comes into play, and what is at stake is the meaning and destiny of individual and collective undertakings.... In opposition to the above-mentioned, widespread conviction of the abstruseness and uselessness of the doctrine of the Trinity, we could say that for the Christian nothing is more vital and concrete than faith in the Trinity of the Father, the Son and the Holy Spirit, in whose name and for whose glory the Christian has been called to be and to do all things.

"The Trinity is a profession of faith in salvation!"[5]

Our entire Christian existence is permeated with the trinitarian mystery, not only on the level of personal existence but also on that of Church and social life. It is not by chance that the banishment of the Trinity from Christian theory and practice is mirrored in the visibilism and legalism that often rule people's conception of the Church, and that there are also socio-political consequences.[6]

Therefore, a return to the "trinitarian homeland" holds promise for both ecclesiology and the entire historical situation of Christianity. This return is perhaps the most burning challenge facing the Church and its theology. "The greatest problem for the Church and the greatest task for theology is that of seeing to it that the Trinity becomes a spiritually vital thought for the be-

liever and for the theologian, that the entire doctrine of the faith and the entire existence of the
believer will be conceived of and lived on the
basis of professed faith in the Trinity. Hence, the
problem is to understand the profession of trinitarian faith as a permanent norm for critiquing
the life of the Church, as a factor in the critique of
earthly life in the world and as an unfailing axiom
in the eschatological measure of history."[7]

This urgency is likewise impelling in regard to
the universal, personal and collective problem of
learning to love in order to attain the truth of life
in love. The person who wants to learn how to
love and who seeks the strength to do so, cannot
tolerate for any length of time the banishment of
love—i.e., the Trinity—from eternal history. Khalil
Gibran intuited this, writing in *The Prophet*: "When
you love, do not say: I have God in my heart, but
rather: I am in God's heart."[8] To be in God's
heart—is this not perhaps "remaining" in the Holy
Spirit, through the Son, under the loving gaze of
the Father?

It is to the sacred account of God's trinitarian
love revealed at Easter that we must turn in order to speak of the Trinity in a way that is concrete and meaningful for us. As intuited in Christian iconography, the Cross and Resurrection
speak of the Trinity, and whoever wishes to tell
the story of God's love must focus on the Cross
and Resurrection in order to make the history of

that love present in the lives of God's people on earth.

It is in the story of Easter that the Trinity offers itself as the source and paradigm of love.

The Icon of the West:
The Cross as Trinitarian History

In the West the Trinity is often represented by an icon of the Crucified Savior, supported by the Father's hands, while the dove of the Spirit both unites and separates the Abandoning One and the Abandoned One. It is the iconographic depiction of a profound theological concept that sees in the Cross the focal point of revelation of the Trinity. The early Church intuited this truth of the Cross as part of the history of the Trinity. We infer this from the space given to the account of the Nazarene's passion and death in the Church's announcement of its origins, for are not the Gospels "histories of the passion with detailed introductions," as well expressed by M. Kahler? But we also infer it from the precise theological structure that underlies the passion narratives.

This structure can be grasped through the constant repetition—certainly not accidental—of the verb "to hand over"[9] or "to give up."

We can distinguish two types of "handing over." The first consists in the succession of actions in which the Galilean prophet is handed over by other persons. The betrayal of love delivers him to his enemies: Judas Iscariot, one of the twelve, goes to the chief priests in order to *hand* Jesus *over* to them (cf Mk 14:10). The Sanhedrin, guardian and representative of the law, delivers the blasphemer to Caesar's representative: "As soon as morning came, the chief priests with the elders and the scribes, that is, the whole Sanhedrin, held a council. They bound Jesus, led him away, and *handed* him *over* to Pilate" (Mk 15:1).

Pilate is convinced of his innocence: "Why? What evil has he done?" (Mk 15:14) But he gives in to the pressure of the crowd, which has been egged on by its leaders (cf 15:11): "So Pilate... released Barabbas...and, after he had Jesus scourged, he *handed* him *over* to be crucified" (Mk 15:15).

Deserted by his followers, considered a blasphemer by the keepers of the law and a subversive by the representative of the civil power, Jesus goes to meet his end. If everything were to stop here, his would be one of so many unjust deaths in history, where an innocent person lays down his life in failure in the face of the world's injustice. But the newly-formed community, marked by the experience of Easter, knows that such is not the case. For this reason, it speaks to us of three other mysterious instances of "handing over."

The first is the *Son's* handing over of himself.

Paul expressed it clearly: "Insofar as I now live in the flesh, I live by faith in the Son of God who has loved me and *given* himself *up* for me" (Gal 2:20; cf 1:4; 1 Tm 2:6; Ti 2:14). "Live in love, as Christ loved us and *handed* himself *over* for us as a sacrificial offering to God for a fragrant aroma" (Eph 5:2; cf 5:25). We note that these expressions correspond to the gospel witness: "Father, into your hands I commend my spirit" (Lk 23:46: quotation from Ps 31:5). "And bowing his head, he *handed over* the spirit" (Jn 19:30).

The Son *hands* himself *over* to God his Father for love of us and in our place, and this handing over is made all the more momentous by the pain of the offering. It is the supreme expression of Jesus' devotion to the Father, and—in the light of Easter—one can see on a finite level the eternal relationship of the infinite gift of himself which the Son lives with God his Father. The journey of the Son toward alienation, his handing over of himself to death, is the projection in God's plan of what takes place in the immanence of the trinitarian mystery.

Through this handing over, the crucified Savior makes history. He takes upon himself the burden of the pain and the sin of the world past, present and future. He enters into uttermost banishment from God, to take the banishment of sinners upon himself in the paschal offering and reconciliation: "Christ ransomed us from the curse of the law, by becoming a curse for us, for it is written, 'Cursed be everyone who hangs on a tree,' that the blessing of Abraham might be extended to the Gentiles through Christ Jesus, so that we might receive the promise of the Spirit through faith" (Gal 3:13-14). Is not the cry of the dying Jesus the sign of the abyss of suffering and of banishment that the Son willed to take upon himself, to enter the depths of the world's suffering and bring it to reconciliation with the Father? "My God, my God, why have you forsaken me?" (Mk 15:34; cf Mt 27:46)[10]

Corresponding to the Son's "handing over" of himself is the *Father's* "handing over." This is already indicated by the formulas of the so-called "divine passive voice": "The Son of Man is to be *handed over* to men, and they will kill him" (Mk 9:31; cf 10:33, 45; Mk 14:41f; Mt 26:45b-46). He will not be handed over by men, by whom he is to be crucified; nor will he hand himself over, for the verb is in the passive voice. It will be God, his Father, who will hand him over: "For God so loved the world that he gave his only Son, so that everyone who believes in him might not perish but might have eternal life" (Jn 3:16).

"He who did not spare his own Son but handed him over for us all, how will he not also give us everything else along with him?" (Rom 8:32) It is in this "handing over" by the Father of his own Son, that we behold the depth of his love for humanity. "In this is love: not that we have loved God but that he loved us and sent his Son as expiation for our sins" (1 Jn 4:10; cf Rom 5:6-11).

The Father, too, makes history in the hour of the Cross. In sacrificing his own Son, he judges the gravity of the sin of the world past, present and future. He also shows the greatness of his merciful love for us. After the "handing over" of wrath ("therefore, God *handed* them *over* to impurity through the lusts of their hearts"—Rom 1:24ff) comes the "handing over" of love! The offering of the Cross reveals in the suffering Father the source of a greater gift, in time and in eternity: the Cross reveals that "God [the Father] is love" (1 Jn 4:8, 16)!

The Father's suffering corresponds to that of the crucified Son as a gift and sacrificial offering and is prefigured by Abraham's suffering in the offering of Isaac, his "only" son (cf Gen 22:12; Jn 3:16 and 1 Jn 4:9). This suffering is nothing but another name for the Father's infinite love. In the Father, as in the Son, the supreme and painful "handing over" is the sign of the supreme love that changes history: "No one has greater love than this, to lay down one's life for one's friends. You are my friends if you do what I command you.... I have called you friends, because I told you everything I have heard from my Father" (Jn 15:13-15).

History of the Father and of the Son, the Cross

is equally the history of the *Spirit*. The supreme act of "handing over" is the sacrificial offering of the Spirit, as understood by John the Evangelist: "Bowing his head, he handed over the spirit" (Jn 19:30). It is "through the eternal Spirit" that Christ "offered himself unblemished to God" (Heb 9:14). Moreover, he who offered himself on the cross is the Anointed One of the Father: "God anointed Jesus of Nazareth with the holy Spirit and power.... They put him to death by hanging him on a tree. This man God raised [on] the third day" (Acts 10:38-40).

At the hour of the Cross, the crucified Savior "hands over" to the Father the Holy Spirit whom the Father has given him and who will be given back to him in fullness on the day of resurrection. Good Friday, the day that the Son hands himself over to the Father and the Father hands over the Son to death for sinners, is the day on which the Spirit is handed over by the Son to his Father, so that the Son will remain alone, far from God the Father, in the company of sinners.[11]

It is the hour of death *in* God, of separation between the Father and the Son, in their eternal, ceaseless communion in the Holy Spirit. It is an event that culminates in the "handing over" of the Spirit himself to the Father. This event makes possible the supreme banishment of the Son into the otherness of the world, his becoming a "curse" in the land of those who have been cursed by

God, so that these persons may enter with him into the joy of the Easter reconciliation.

Without the handing over of the Spirit, the Cross would not appear in all its radicality as a trinitarian and saving event. If the Spirit had not let himseLf be handed over in the silence of death, with all the torment that this entailed, the hour of darkness could be misunderstood as the unthinkable death *of* God, as the incomprehensible quenching of the Absolute. It would not be understood as it actually is: as an act that takes place *in* God, an event in the history of the love of the immortal God, in which the Son, obedient to the Father, enters into the most profound alienation from him—enters into the company of sinners. Out of love the Father delivers the Son into this supreme exile, so that on the eschatological day of Easter ("the third day") those who have been exiled from God may return, with, in and through the Son, to communion with the Father: "For our sake he made him to be sin who did not know sin, so that we might become the righteousness of God in him" (2 Cor 5:21; cf Rom 8:3).

"However great the separation of sinful humanity from God may seem, it is always less profound than the Son's separation from the Father in his kenotic emptying (cf Phil 2:7) and the misery of being 'forsaken' (Mt 27:46). In the economy of the redemption, this is the precise aspect proper to the distinction of the Persons of the Holy Trinity, who nonetheless are perfectly united in the identity of a single nature and infinite love."[12]

The handing over of the Spirit expresses the Son's banishment in obedience to the Father's handing over of him, and, therefore, the salvation made possible to the alienated, in the company of the crucified Savior. At the hour of the Cross, then, the Holy Spirit himself makes history: history in God, because, in being handed over to the Father, the Spirit makes it possible for the Son to be alienated from the Father in solidarity with sinners, yet in the infinite communion expressed by the crucified Savior's sacrificial obedience. This is *our* history, because it has brought the Son close to us, permitting the alienated to follow the Son out of exile toward the homeland of trinitarian and paschal communion.

As the history of the Son, of the Father and of the Holy Spirit, the Cross is the trinitarian history of God: "In the Cross erected on Golgotha, the eternal heart of the Trinity has been made manifest."[13] "The theology of 'handing over' can be thoroughly understood only in a trinitarian sense."[14] "What was traditionally called 'vicarious expiation' must be understood, transformed and exalted as a trinitarian mystery."[15]

The trinitarian figure offers itself on the cross in the unity of the Father, who hands over the Son, of the Son, who hands himself over, of the

Holy Spirit, handed over by the Son and received by the Father. "If we understand the Cross of Jesus as an event of God, as an event that involves God the Father as well as God the Son, we will be impelled to speak in a trinitarian manner of the Father, the Son and the Holy Spirit. Therefore, the trinitarian doctrine is not a free speculation about God, devoid of any practicality, but rather the compendium of the history of Christ's passion with the meaning it takes on for the eschatological freedom of the faith and life of burdened nature.... The content of trinitarian doctrine is the real Cross of Christ. The form of the crucified Savior is the Trinity."[16]

The Cross states, therefore, that the Trinity makes its own the exile of a world subject to sin, so that with Easter that exile may enter the homeland of trinitarian communion. The Cross is our history because it is the trinitarian history of God. It does not proclaim the blasphemy of a death *of* God, which makes room for each person to live imprisoned in self-sufficiency, but rather it proclaims the good news of death *in* God, so that each person may live the life of the immortal God, participating in the trinitarian communion— a participation which that saving death made possible.

On the Cross, the "homeland" enters into exile, so that exile may enter into the "homeland." In this we are offered the key of history! "The 'history of

God,' brought into our reality by the death of Jesus on the cross at Golgotha, contains every breadth and depth of human history and can be understood as the history of histories. All human history, though marked by sin and death, is taken up into this 'history of God,' that is, into the Trinity, and will be integrated into the future 'history of God'!"[17]

Thus, the Cross brings one to Easter: the hour of hiatus points to the hour of reconciliation, the sway of death to the triumph of life! The Son's alienation from the Father on Good Friday, culminating in the painful handing over of the Spirit, his "descending into hell," to be in solidarity with all those who were, are and will be prisoners of sin and death—all this is directed to the reunion of the Son with the Father through the paschal mystery. This takes place on the "third day," through the Father's gift of the Spirit to the Son and in and through him to sinful humankind, which is thus reconciled: "But now in Christ Jesus you who once were far off have become near by the blood of Christ. For he is our peace.... Through him we both have access in one Spirit to the Father" (Eph 2:13, 14, 18).

The alienation of the Cross is followed by the communion of the Resurrection, in God and for the world! "Only if we recognize from the start the trinitarian dimension of the event can we speak adequately of 'for us' and 'for the world.'

On the one hand, in the contrast of the Father's will and the Son's will in the garden of olives and in the Father's abandonment of the Son on the cross, we behold the highest economic opposition between the divine Persons. On the other hand, for a person who reflects deeply, it is precisely this opposition that constitutes the ultimate manifestation of God's entire unified saving action, whose intrinsic consequences are in turn manifested in the inseparability of the death on the cross and the Resurrection."[18]

Death in God for the world on Good Friday becomes the world's life in God on Easter. For it is not the death of sin but death in love; it is the death of death, which does not torment, but reconciles, does not negate God's oneness, but eminently affirms it in itself and for the world.

The Icon of the East:
The Resurrection as Trinitarian History

If on the cross the Son "handed over" the Spirit to the Father, plunging himself into the abyss of alienation from God—in the Resurrection the Father gives the Spirit to the Son, embracing the world in him and with him in infinite divine communion. This is the intuition that underlies the way the Trinity is often depicted in Eastern iconography. The set of three angelic figures placed around the banquet cup has a dynamism that carries through to the person who contemplates the icon. The onlooker, in turn, becomes an icon of the Trinity, a reflection of trinitarian life in time, thanks to the paschal outpouring of the Spirit, brought about through the banquet of the Risen One.

The early Church testified to all this through its narration of the Resurrection as trinitarian history. The texts fully confirm that Christ was resurrected,[19] that "God raised him up" (Acts 2:24—the formula is repeated continually in the Acts). The initiative in the Resurrection is taken by God the Father. This is the powerful action of the "Father of glory," who shows "the surpassing greatness of his power," "the exercise of his great might" (Eph 1:17, 19). The Father makes history, because he takes a stand in regard to the Crucified One, declaring him to be Lord and Christ: "God has made him both Lord and Messiah, this Jesus whom you crucified" (Acts 2:36).

In the light of the double meaning of these titles—theological and soteriological[20]—we understand how the Father's act authorizes us to recognize in the Nazarene's past, the history of God's Son among men; in his present, the Living One, Conqueror of death; and in his future, the Lord who will return in glory. In the Resurrection, God actively presents himself as the Father of the Incarnate Son, who is alive for us and will come on the Last Day.

At the same time, on Easter Day the Father takes a stand on the history of humankind. In regard to the past, he judges the triumph of evil that took place on the cross of the Humiliated One, declaring "no" to the sin of the world: "Despoiling the principalities and powers, he made a public spectacle of them, leading them away in triumph..." (Col 2:15). In regard to the present, he offers himself as the God and Father of mercy, who in his "yes" to the Crucified One pronounces his liberating "yes" to all those enslaved by sin and death: "God, who is rich in mercy, because of the great love he had for us, even when we were dead in our transgressions, brought us to life with Christ...[and] raised us up with him" (Eph 2:4-6; cf Rom 5:8; Col 2:13, etc.) In regard to our future, he presents himself as the God of the promise, who has faithfully fulfilled "what he had announced beforehand through the mouth of all the prophets" and who guarantees the times of consolation, when he will again send his Anointed Jesus (cf Acts 3:18-20). As the history of the Father, the Resurrection is therefore the great "yes" that the God of life says to his Son and, in him, to us, the prisoners of death. Therefore, it is the theme of the Good News and the foundation of the Faith, capable of giving meaning and hope to our activity and life: "If Christ has not been raised, then empty [too] is our preaching; empty, too, your faith" (1 Cor 15:14).

History of the Father, the Resurrection is also the history of the *Son*. There is ample evidence for the tradition that states: "Christ is risen" (cf Mk 16:6; Mt 27:64; 28:67; Lk 24:6, 34; 1 Thes 4:14; 1 Cor 15:3-5; Rom 8:34; Jn 21:14; etc.). The pre-Easter Jesus declares: "Destroy this temple, and in three days I will raise it up," and the evangelist comments: "he was speaking about the temple of his body" (Jn 2:19, 21). This active role of the Son in the paschal mystery in no way contradicts the Father's initiative. "If in the Son's extreme obedience it is fitting that he should let himself be raised up by the Father, it pertains in no less a way to the fulfillment of his obedience that he should let himself be 'given' by the Father 'the possession of life in himself' (cf Jn 5:26)."[21]

The proclamation that Jesus is Lord is always "to the glory of God the Father" (Phil 2:11)! Christ therefore rises from the dead, actively taking a stand concerning his history and that of humankind for whom he offered himself to death. If his Cross is the triumph of sin, the Law and power, because he was "handed over" by unfaithfulness in love (the handing over by Judas—cf Mk 14:10), by the hatred of the representatives of the Law (the handing over by the Sanhedrin—cf Mk 15:1), and by the authority of Caesar's representative (the handing over by Pilate—cf Mk 15:11), his Resurrection is the defeat of power, the Law and sin. It is the triumph of freedom, grace and love.

In him who rises, life overcomes death. The "abandoned one," the "blasphemer," the "revolutionary" is the Lord of Life (cf Rom 5:12–7:25: the liberation from sin, death and the Law brought about by Christ). Regarding the past, the Risen One has confirmed his pre-Easter claim by shaming the wise (cf 1 Cor 1:23ff) and has broken down the dividing wall of hostility, the fruit of iniquity (cf Eph 2:14-18). Regarding the present, he shows himself as the Living One (cf Acts 1:3) and the giver of life (cf Jn 20:21). Regarding the future, he is the Lord of glory, the first fruits of the new humanity (cf 1 Cor 15:20-28). Easter is the history of the Son, and for this reason it is also *our* history, since the Risen One has overcome death for us and has given us life.

Finally, the Resurrection is the history of the *Holy Spirit*. It is in his power that Christ has been raised: "Put to death in the flesh, he was brought to life in the spirit" (1 Pt 3:18). Jesus was designated by the Father as "Son of God in power according to the Spirit of holiness through resurrection from the dead" (Rom 1:4). The Spirit is above all he who has been given by the Father to the Son so that the Humbled One may be exalted and the Crucified One may live the new life of him who has risen. At the same time, the Spirit is the one whom the Lord Jesus gives according to his promise (cf Jn 14:16; 15:26; 16:7): "God raised this Jesus; of this we are all witnesses. Exalted at the right hand of God, he received the promise of the Holy Spirit from the Father and poured it forth, as you [both] see and hear" (Acts 2:33).

Thus, the Holy Spirit holds a place in the paschal event, for he is the twofold bond between the Father and Christ, and between the Risen One and us. He brings together the Father and the Son, raising Jesus from the dead; he unites God's people with the Risen Christ, making them alive with new life. He guarantees the twofold identity in the contradiction experienced by those who have lived the paschal event. He makes the Crucified One the Living One; he makes the prisoners of fear and death become free and courageous witnesses of life and love. He is not the Father, because he is given by the Father. He is not the Son, because the Risen One receives him and gives him. He is Someone who, never separated from the Father and Son, is distinct and independent in his action, as is attested, for example, by the missionary mandate to baptize "in the name of the Father, and of the Son, and of the Holy Spirit" (Mt 28:19) or from this greeting, which is probably of liturgical origin: "The grace of the Lord Jesus Christ and the love of God and the fellowship of the Holy Spirit be with all of you" (2 Cor 13:14).

As the history of the Father, Son and Holy Spirit, the Resurrection of Jesus from the dead is therefore an event in God's trinitarian history. In this the Trinity presents itself as the unity of the resurrecting Father, the resurrected Son, and the Spirit of resurrection and life, given and received—the unity of the God of the fathers, who in his Spirit gives life to the Crucified, proclaiming him Lord and Christ, the Son of God and the Risen One, who, receiving the Spirit from the Father, gives him to us so that we may share in the communion of life in the Spirit with the Son and the Father. In the Resurrection, the Trinity presents itself in the unity of a twofold movement from the Father in the Spirit to the Son, and from the Father through the Son in the Spirit to humanity, that is, in the unity of Christ's Resurrection and of our new life in him. The paschal event reveals the unity of the Trinity open to us in love, and therefore it is the offer of salvation—of full participation in the life of the Father, of the Son and of the Holy Spirit. The Trinity, the trinitarian history of God revealed at Easter, is the history of salvation—our history.

The Trinity as Love's History: The Eternal Love Story

The paschal event reveals the trinitarian history *of God*. It is not only the history of the Father, the Son and the Holy Spirit as revealed in the fruitfulness of their reciprocal relations and in their marvelous free gift of their love to the world.

The paschal event also reveals the unfathomable oneness of the Three who made history: oneness amid ineradicable differences (the Cross) and in the deepest communion (the Resurrection). They are one in the story that Love (the Father) hands over the Beloved One (the Son). Allowing himself be delivered up in absolute freedom, and being handed over so that the divine can enter into the exile of sinners, the Son is completely "poured out" at the paschal moment to bring about the entrance of sinners into the unifying and lifegiving home of divine love (the Spirit).

The oneness of the paschal event is the oneness of the love that loves (the Father), that is loved (the Son), that unites both in freedom (the Spirit—cf 1 Jn 4:7-16). At Easter, this is shown as the love that not only produces and creates unity but already presupposes it, not so much a union of separate persons as a reunion of Persons who were separated from one another out of love for the world and who from the exile of alienation return to the original yet new oneness of their eternal love.[22]

Moreover, the entire mission and work of Jesus of Nazareth unfold in the sign of his preexisting and eternal oneness with the Father and the Holy Spirit. He who receives and gives the Spirit (cf Jn 1:33) is the Son of God (cf Jn 1:34), one with the Father (cf Jn 10:30). Through his paschal mystery he calls for and establishes the unity of all people in God's trinitarian oneness: "In that day [when the Spirit will be poured out—cf verses 16 and 17] you will realize that I am in my Father and you are in me and I in you.... Whoever loves me will be loved by my Father, and I will love him and manifest myself to him.... Whoever loves me will keep my word, and my Father will love him and we will come to him and make our dwelling with him" (Jn 14:20-21, 23) "...that they may all be one, as you, Father, are in me and I in you, that they also may be in us, that the world may believe that you sent me.... I in them and you in me, that they may be brought to perfection as one, so that the world may know that you sent me and that you loved them even as you loved me" (Jn 17:21, 23).

It is to this living oneness of the Triune God that we have access through baptism. We have to take into account the Semitic meaning of the word "name," which means the living essence. To be baptized "in the *name* of the Father and of the Son and of the Holy Spirit" (Mt 28:19), means to enter into the unique mystery of their being, of their unfathomable oneness.

How should we understand this trinitarian one-ness, revealed and communicated at Easter? Where and how can we begin to contemplate the mystery, so that from the outward activity of God we can—as far as possible—reach the imma-nence of the divine oneness? The faith of the

Church has defended this oneness of God against those who wanted to deny or dissolve it. The statement of the Council of Nicea (325) on the "consubstantiality" of the Son with the Father declares, against Arian subordinationism, that they are on the same level of divine being; they are one in divinity, of one and the same "essence."[23]

Against the Pneumatomachi, who subordinated the Holy Spirit to Christ, the Council of Constantinople (831) affirms the same equality in divine being of the Holy Spirit with the Father and the Son, with whom "he is adored and glorified" as the "Lord and giver of life."[24] The creed formula *Quicumque* clearly declares: "The Catholic faith is that we worship one sole God in trinity, and trinity in oneness, without confusing the Persons and without dividing the substance: one Person is that of the Father, another is that of the Son, and another that of the Holy Spirit, but one and only is the divinity of the Father, the Son and the Holy Spirit, equal in glory, coeternal in majesty."[25] "Nor, in confessing three Persons, do we acknowledge three substances, but only one single substance and three Persons."[26]

From the perspective of the world of thought, this divine oneness was first defended and formulated conceptually in order to express in words the experience of the unity of the event of salvation. It was therefore conceived as oneness of "essence" or "substance" or divine "nature." These terms tell "what something is," "what lies underneath." To affirm that the Three have one sole "essence" or "substance" or "nature" is therefore to affirm the oneness of their divine being, their perfect equality in terms of divinity, and hence their being one, sole God. Their oneness is thus expressed in the most radical way, as oneness of being, as ontological oneness.[27]

Within that oneness, the three Persons are distinguished by their reciprocal relationships, by that (relative) otherness in (essential) identity which is "subsistent relationship": "person" in God.[28] This interpretation may thoroughly safeguard divine oneness, but it risks focusing attention on the essential dimensions rather than the personal life of the divinity. Therefore, in speaking of the Christian God, this interpretation stresses that essentialism which, biblically speaking, leaves something to be desired. This is no secondary cause of the forgetful omission of the Trinity from Christian theory and practice.

The Christian God is not "just any" God, but is properly and specifically the Triune God. Christian monotheism is not one among others, but it is trinitarian monotheism! It is this aspect that the development of thought, above all in the West, has underplayed, even though in expressing the Faith there is no doubt that the formula of the single essence or substance or divine nature of the Three corresponds precisely to the datum of revelation in categories that differ from the historical-narrative categories of the original paschal announcement.

To overcome the essentialism of classical thought, there has been a trend in modern times— even in trinitarian theology—to make new use of subjectivity. Thus, beginning with Hegel, the unity of the Triune God has been interpreted as the unity of the one divine Subject in the eternal history of the Spirit. God the Father is self-differentiated in God the Son and self-identified in the Holy Spirit. This conception introduces the movement of life and history into the concept of God, and therefore it appears closer to the living image of God found in revelation. In reality, however, this completely drains the personal Trinity, breaking it down into the "becoming" of the one divine Subject, assimilated into the "total becoming" of world history. The Hegelian monism of the Spirit is no less removed from Christian monotheism than any other indeterminate monotheism!

To overcome the risks of "mad" essentialism and the snare of subjectivity, the oneness of the Christian God may be interpreted according to historical thinking. Divine oneness is conceived not as a static essence but as dynamism, process, life, as a history of trinitarian love. From the revelation of love that is Loving, Beloved and Unify-

ing in freedom—which is the paschal mystery—
we can say that the divine oneness, or if we wish,
the one and only divine essence (dynamically
understood), is love: the one God is Love, in the
ineradicable trinitarian differentiation of the Loving One, of personal Love.

This is the line of thought already glimpsed by
Augustine, even though he did not follow it all
the way,[29] perhaps owing to the influence of
essentialism predominant in the thinking of his
time: "In truth, if you see love, you see the Trinity."[30] "They are three in number: the Loving
One, the Beloved, and Love."[31] "And they are not
more than three: One who loves him who comes
from himself, One who loves him from whom he
comes, and Love itself.... And if this is nothing, in
what way *is God love?* And if this is not substance, in what way is God substance?"[32] To
"speak of God's being cannot and must not mean
other than to speak of God's love."[33] "God is
love. God is not only *in* love, as those who love
one another are *in* love. God is not only I who
love and you who are loved. God is, rather, the
radiant event of Love itself. He is such... not only
loving himself but always more forgetful of self,
however great his love of self may be—a distinct
"you," and *thus* he is and remains himself. God
possesses himself in giving himself, and only in
giving himself. But in this way, in giving himself,
he possesses himself. Thus he *is*. His possession

of himself is the event, the history of self-giving and in this sense the goal of any mere self-possession. As this *history*, he is God; rather, this story of love is 'God himself.'"[34]

The essence of the living God is therefore his love in an eternal movement: of self-emptying, as loving Love; of self-acceptance, as loved Love; of return to self and infinite openness to the other in freedom, as Spirit of trinitarian love. The essence of the Christian God is love in its eternal process; it is the trinitarian history of love; it is the Trinity as the eternal history of love, who enlivens and embraces and pervades the history of the world, the object of God's pure love.

The paschal event does not reveal the divine essence as anything other than the eternal event of love between the Three and of their love for us. "Only this movement of love constitutes the divine essence, so that only in the three divine relations—the Father who loves in and of himself, the Son who is loved and always loves, and the ever new event of love between Father and Son, which is the Spirit—does it become possible to think of complete identity between the divine essence and existence. The concept of the Triune God, who is love, therefore implies eternal newness, and accordingly, the eternal God is his own future. God and love never grow old. Their being is, and remains, in becoming."[35]

God's oneness is therefore the oneness of his

being-love, of his essential love, which exists eternally as loving Love, loved Love and personal Love or, in other words, as the eternal starting point, arrival point and summit of love;[36] the origin, acceptance and gift of himself; fatherhood, sonship and opening in freedom; Father, Son and Holy Spirit.

This concept of the divine essence as the eternal history of love is linked to the concept of trinitarian *perichoresis*. Derived from such texts as John 10:38—"The Father is in me and I am in the Father" (cf Jn 14:9ff; 17:21; etc.)—the expression is meant to convey the mutual compenetration (hence the Latin *circumincessio*) and mutual indwelling (hence also, *circuminsessio*) of the divine Persons, the inexhaustible movement of trinitarian life, its self-unfolding and convergence in love. Thus is it illustrated by St. John Damascene—who seems to have been the first person to introduce the term: "The remaining and abiding of the three Persons within one another signifies that they are inseparable and not detached and have between them a compenetration without confusion, not in such a way that they fuse or mingle, but in such a way that they are united.... The movement is one and identical, since the vitality and dynamism of the three Persons is unique, something we cannot say about created nature."[37]

The magnificence of this vision, which is proper

to the East but not restricted to it,[38] lies in the fact that it refutes every concept of the Trinity that pushes to extremes either the oneness (modalism) or the personal distinction (tritheism). It shows that in God the unity and the individuality of the Persons not only do not compete but reciprocally affirm one another. As Love, the divine essence does not exclude the personal differentiations, but includes them. This holds true both for the immanence of the divine life (trinitarian *perichoresis*) and for the mystery of this life shared with human beings (divine-human relationship and ecclesial communion).

True love never cancels out differences, even if it gathers them into a more profound unity.... In this light we may also reread the principle of *opus Dei ad extra indivisum*—i.e., the undivided divine action with respect to creatures. It is a consequence of the fact that "in God everything is one, except where there is an opposition of relations."[39] This cannot mean that the divine action *ad extra* is undifferentiated, as though when God turns to his creatures, beginning from the act of creation, the personal properties of the Father, Son and Holy Spirit disappear. Such would conflict with the specific account of salvation history, so much so that even from a more rigorously essentialistic perspective there was felt to be a need to work out a theology of "appropriations,"[40] which agrees to associate essential attributes to the individual divine Persons, through which the properties that the Persons have in the immanence of the mystery are better manifested in the divine economy.

Divine action *ad extra*, then, is to be understood in a "perichoretic" sense—i.e., in the light of the living dynamism of the divine oneness. This means that the Father does nothing without corresponding action from the Son and Spirit; the Word does nothing without the Father and the Spirit; and the Spirit does nothing without the Father and the Son. Hence, every act of trinitarian love toward creatures implies the differentiation of the Loving One, the Beloved and Personal Love, in their unfathomable oneness: the *opus ad extra* is always an *opus amoris* [work of love], in which the three Persons are present and involved, each One according to his own properties. Love is never indifference!

Consequently, there is no salvific experience of a divine Person that does not involve an encounter with the whole Trinity. No "christomonism" or "pneumatomonism" is admissible, nor a unilateral absolutizing of only one divine Person. Nor can we speak of an abstract, undifferentiated monotheism, but only that monotheism which respects the movements toward otherness and fellowship in the unfathomable oneness of love which is God's eternal history. Only such a concept of the one God, which is trinitarian monotheism, shows humanity the face of the Christian

God, who is always Father, Son and Spirit, in the oneness of divine love, in itself and for us. Only trinitarian monotheism speaks of God by *telling the story* of Love.

The History of the Trinity: The Trinity as Origin, Womb and Home of the Story of Love

A human person's decision for Christ opens temporal existence to the acceptance of eternal life: in the story of the present, the eternal love story is told. How does this transition take place? How do human beings, in whom the image of the Holy Trinity is imprinted, enter into the very life of the Trinity? And how does the Trinity enter in a new and full way into the lives of creatures?

From the very beginning of the Christian Faith, the decisive act of this transition was embodied and celebrated in baptism in the name of the Trinity: "Go, therefore, and make disciples of all nations, baptizing them in the name of the Father, and of the Son, and of the Holy Spirit" (Mt 28:19). Christian existence is a baptismal existence, and since the paschal mystery is represented in baptism, and the Trinity is named and given, this existence is paschal, trinitarian. The liturgy expresses this mystery by uniting baptism in a special way to the Easter Vigil and by stressing the confession of faith that is asked of baptismal candidates in the three questions that refer respectively to the Father, to the Son and to the Holy Spirit, and to their role in salvation history.

Thus, the divine life of the three Persons, their "nature" (cf 2 Pt 1:4), is communicated to the life of the person who is baptized. The eternal story of their love is narrated in time. The new life in baptism comes from the Father, through assimilation to Christ, crucified and risen, in the grace of the Holy Spirit. It is a life that reflects the oneness of the Trinity by incorporation into the mystical body of Christ (cf Eph 4:4ff) and by anticipation of the future unity of God's Kingdom.

Baptismal existence is therefore rooted and grounded in the Trinity and expresses itself in a dynamism that involves an analogy to the life of the Godhead. From the very beginning, this expression of paschal existence, inserted into the mystery of the Trinity through baptism, has been embodied in the theological life of faith, hope and love (cf 1 Thes 1:3; 5:8; 1 Cor 13:7, 13; Gal 5:5ff; Rom 5:1-5; 12:6-12; Col 1:4ff; Eph 1:15-18; 4:2-5; etc.). In the Trinity the Christian is a person of faith and hope, a person in love!

Since through baptism each person is related to God the Father as his adopted son or daughter and restored image (cf Col 3:10; Rom 8:29; 1 Cor 15:49; 2 Cor 3:18), everyone reflects in himself or herself what is proper to the Father: to be a wellspring of love, to be loving. This reflection in the person and in his or her history is *charity*. It is the greatest gift, because it relates the person to the origin and beginning of all things and of all love (cf 1 Cor 13:13). It inspires and gives validity to every initiative to do good (cf 1 Cor 13:1-6). It is at the root of faith and hope, for "it believes all things" and "hopes all things" (1 Cor 13:7).

Thanks to charity, persons can love with an effusion, generosity and creativity that they would not have on their own; these are communicated to them by the Father. "Where there are charity and love, *God* is there." In the love of charity, baptismal existence makes God himself present and "visible"!

Since through baptism a person is incorporated into the Incarnate Son, in this paschal existence one reflects in oneself what is proper to the Son: to be receptive to love, to be loved. This response is *faith*. It is the acceptance of God's gift. It is loving obedience, faithful listening to the Word (cf for instance, Rom 1:5; 6:17; 10:7; 2 Cor 10:4; 1 Tm 1:6; 2 Tm 1:8; etc.).

Believers participate in a certain way in the eternal movement of love, through which the Son totally accepts the Father's love and eternally becomes his Image. In this sense, believing is letting oneself be loved by God, "letting oneself become a prisoner of the Invisible" (Luther). Faith does not seek guarantees. It makes no contracts and does not calculate: it accepts, trusts and obeys. Thus, the object of faith, Christ, is also the model of our faith—he who has gone before us in the battle of faith (cf Heb 12:2).[41]

The mystery of the Son's obedience is represented in the life of the believer: one's very theological existence is totally a received existence! In short, insofar as a person is filled with the gift of the Holy Spirit through baptism, he or she reflects in theological life what is proper to the Spirit: to be a bond of unity and openness to freedom in love. In our baptismal existence, this reflection is *hope*. It unites the present to God's future, ever opening the heart of the believer to what is coming and what is new.

Far from denoting passive expectation or sterile escapism, theological hope is an active anticipation of the future promise; it is "a passion for what is possible" (S. Kierkegaard), which brings God's tomorrow into our today. Hope gives imagination to the outpouring of love and courage to the obedience of faith!

These reflections justify an inquiry regarding the relationship between the Trinity, origin of history, and the human community. If God the Creator wills the complete fulfillment of his human creatures and if this can be achieved only in the social life of love, there has to be a relation between the eternal story of the trinitarian communion and the historical process of the upbuilding of the human family. We can discern this bond in regard to each of the divine Persons in their relationship of love with one another.

Even as the trinitarian communion derives from the *Father*, the eternal fountain of love, the community of the human family is related constitutively to God the Father, the Lord of heaven and earth. This means that it is a *communion in love of various "springs,"* which must unite to become *one wellspring of life and love.*

A community will not reflect the Father if within it there is no respect for each person's dignity, for his or her independent creativity in the initiative of love, and for his or her original and inimitable being. Neither will a community reflect the Father if these differing original features within it do not converge into a communion, to become a common and greater wellspring for all. That this may not be done under the banner of one person's will and domination over another's, and hence through authoritarian and oppressive forms, is required by the fact that such a way of building a community would contradict the original character placed by the Creator in the depths of each human person. Far from being a "universal monarch" who justifies despotic rule on earth, God, the Father of the Trinity, calls each person to be himself or herself, and as such to respect everyone else's dignity and identity as a source of love.

We can acknowledge that "the affirmation of

the one God and in particular of his attributes of absoluteness and omnipotence, apart from our profession of faith in the Trinity, lends itself— and in the history of Christianity has often lent itself—to serve as a theological support for political and ecclesial structures under the banner of one person's domination and will over another."[42]

Although the inference "One God, one Lord, one people, one kingdom" corresponds to a Greek longing for the One (according to which "human beings do not want to be badly governed: it is not good to have several rulers; let there be only one ruler"),[43] such an inference is diametrically opposed to the Christian image of God the Father and his reflection in history. It is no less opposed to the God of the prophetic monotheism of the Old Testament, in whom the paschal Church has recognized the countenance of the trinitarian Father.

God is not a cold omnipotence that justifies absolute power for anyone on earth. "What is omnipotent is only his love, passionate and capable of suffering." Therefore, "the One and Triune God does not correspond to a sovereign monarch, but rather to a communion among human beings in which privileges and subjection are not recognized."[44]

A community that reflects the face of the Eternal Lover develops to the maximum the precious originality of each person, in a communion greater than the sum of everyone's gifts—a fruitful source of love and life for all, and potentially, of each person's capacity to love.

Even as an individual person is related to the *Son*, in that the person welcomes and receives love, and, in the Son, is the image of the Father, so the community of humankind is called to be the focal point of welcome, where one person welcomes another, and all welcome each. *As a communion of mutual acceptance in love*, the community is a *welcome* more profound than the simple sum of individuals' mutual acceptance. The acceptance of the Son found its highest expression in obedience to the Father, to the point of death on the cross, where he let himself be handed over out of love for sinners. So the community's acceptance must be expressed in a readiness to welcome others, those different from itself, to the point of making a sacrificial gift of itself.

An authentically human community must welcome each person not because of that person's merits, but simply because of the person's existence, respecting what he or she is, accepting the uniqueness and even the "nothingness" of each one. In this sense, a community is truly human and reflects in itself the face of the Son of God when it accepts those who are lost and courageously rejects any discrimination based on power, wealth, race, sex or culture. "In the Cross of Jesus, understood in the light of his life as obedience to the Father and to him alone, God's mystery reveals itself as a full manifestation of his divine love for us and his sharing in our defeated and sinful condition. God's mystery reveals itself as eternally victorious over any domination of one person by another and over all legalism; it also reveals itself as the foundation of a beginning of communal action to serve those who are least."[45]

This radical receptivity of the human community signifies its permanent openness to new and future realities. Nothing of the present moment may be worshiped and no complacency in possessions is allowed, even in the security of a political (or ecclesiastical) ideologically absolutized order.

Welcoming must be lived within the permanent dynamic of the temporary. "The acknowledgment that Jesus is the Truth of God and the Judgment of history, and that we must approach him only in the Spirit, prevents us from absolutizing any ecclesiastical mediation or political order, not only in memory but also in expectation. In fact, neither one nor the other can be identified with God's Kingdom; nor can any social or political order be presented (abstractly or concretely) as the best possible one on earth. Trinitarian faith thus confines the all-embracing demands of any project within the lowliness of life's passing concerns."[46]

Lastly, inasmuch as the person who is in the *Spirit* is God's image because of his or her ability to unite with others and to give freely of self—since the Spirit in the bosom of the Trinity is the bond of unity and is openness in Love—the community of humankind will reflect the Spirit's action. The human community will be a *communion in reciprocity and in the permanent tension of freedom*. A wealth of individual gifts does not constitute a community unless the solitude or isolation of each person is overcome through mutual sharing, which gives rise to communion. This is not the work of ideologies that theoretically reconcile differences, but of love which is received and transmitted from one to another: "The gift of the Holy Spirit places us, not before the Trinity, but within the diversity and reciprocity of the three Persons. Thanks to this gift, trinitarian faith can be distinguished from ideological interpretations that make its historical and political meaning ambiguous."[47]

The communion thus brought about must be expressed in a permanent journey of liberation, by divising social projects that focus on the various needs of the community of mankind in the light of the Trinity. These projects should be continually examined and renewed at the school of history and of fidelity to God, Creator and Savior, so that the decidedly great difficulties entailed in "mediation" will be undergone without easy ideological gains or faithless flight from the struggle. "The revelation of the mystery of God as gift and communion calls for social projects that accept and make the most of persons' gifts and talents and their vocation to mutual sharing. The trinitarian mystery, however, is not set before these projects as a general or even definite model of unity and diversity. The Trinity is not such a model. Precisely, this mystery calls for such undertakings to be enlightened in fidelity to the unmistakable identity of the Father, of the Son and of the Holy Spirit, and of their work in salvation history."[48]

The Trinity is not a formula that can be converted by simple analogical deduction. It is more accurately a horizon that transcends us, a home to return again and again, a love story into which to be inserted—a story to be told through choices of justice and freedom in the days and deeds of humankind.

This is how the image of God in human persons extends to the whole human family—not only to the nuclear family in its relationships of mutual sharing and communion,[49] but also to the entire community of human beings and its history, which are to become a reflection of the divine process of love. And, while all violence and systems of dependence and oppression, exploitation and injustice, obscure the original relationship of creative love, everything that is peace, liberation and justice is an image of and sharing in the trinitarian story of love. The eternal is thus narrated in time through small gestures of solidarity, reconciliation, freedom given and received, passion for justice that is stronger than any defeat....

Origin, womb and home of love, the Trinity makes possible and masterfully molds the humble stories of charity that take place daily within the community of humankind. It makes itself a true wellspring and paradigm of that charity which, in its fully conscious and complete expression, is called to be the Church.

2. The Dialogue of Love

In the journey from death to life, which is an exodus from humanity's earthly existence, there is a point where the human exodus enters intensely into the divine "advent"—an "advent" that is fulfilled in the poverty of the human condition. This point, which is a foretaste of eternity, is love. Is not love perhaps the original and originating experience of every life that is truly lived? And does not the effort of loving constitute the bread of sorrows and tears that is broken so abundantly in anyone's life?

Above all, then, theology, the *wisdom of love*, is an account of love, which appeared to us in the paschal event. A theologian is someone who speaks of God, who speaks of love. And since the story of that crucified Love is also and inseparably a story of the eternal communication of the love of the three Persons ("the recounted history of the Holy Trinity"[1]), telling the story of love will mean recounting the endless communication of divine charity, so as to stimulate and foster a style and practice of dialogue in the lives of believers for the life of the world.

The specific foundation of a *theology of dialogue* is nothing other than a theology of love. In the light of the revealed mystery of divine communication, the theology of love rereads the human condition in its basic communicative structure, as well as in the effort and endeavors involved in the historical realization of this structure. Only in this way will communication be rooted as an indispensable requirement of the human and Christian vocation, outside of any moralizing exhortation or any purely tactical or strategic interpretation of that communication.

a) "To death, the keystone of creation, which single-handedly imprints upon all created beings the indelible mark of finitude, the word has 'gone out.' Love declares war against death—love, which knows only the present, lives in the present and ardently desires the present.... Love is always and completely in 'today,' but in due course every dead 'yesterday' and every dead 'tomorrow' is engulfed by this victorious 'today.' This love is the eternal victory over death. Creation, which death crowns and destroys, cannot hold its own against love; it must surrender to love at every moment and, therefore, in the end, also in the fullness of all moments, in eternity."[2]

Truly, "it is love that gives existence" (M. Blondel). "To love someone means to tell that person: You shall not die!" (G. Marcel). Love is radiant, expansive, the first and always new origin of all life, of every emergence from death. For love we are born; for love we live; to be loved is the joy of life; not to be loved and not to know how to love is infinite sadness.

"Whoever does not love remains in death" (1 Jn 3:14); he or she is not born to life. Love is the *original and originating experience* of existence. It is the original exodus, which is at the same time the mysterious and original advent of the gift of existence. "If I have any unshakable certitude, it is this: a world deserted by love must give way to death, but where love prevails, and where it triumphs over everything that seeks to degrade it, death is definitely overcome."[3]

If this is true, if the most profound of all beings is love, then the sign of love's presence is language, the path of expression and the bridge of communication. The original structure of everything that exists implies the dialectic of diversity and communion, which is the dialectic of love. It takes at least two to love. One comes out of oneself to move toward and welcome the other, rediscovering oneself in that person.

"Love is distinction and the subordination of what is distinct."[4] One who loves recognizes the other as other and tends to become one with that person, not suppressing the otherness but offering one's own identity and accepting as a gift the identity of the other person. Love is an exodus without return, a radical self-offering; love is an advent without regrets, the radical acceptance of the other person.

Therefore, the interplay of being, which is the interplay of love, involves an origin, an arrival and a summit. The origin is always a free offering, an emergence from oneself in the pure generosity of gift, for the sole joy of loving. The arrival is the acceptance of the origin from another, the pure gratitude of letting oneself be loved. The summit is a conversion of the parties: gift becomes welcome and welcome becomes gift; one is freed from self in order to be one with and in the other; a communion is formed, so that the parties can live in new freedom with respect to one another and, together, with respect to others. "Love is not just standing and looking into each other's eyes, but looking together toward the same goal" (A. de Saint-Exupery). Only someone who fully lives this interplay of the origin, arrival and summit of love—only someone who goes through the challenging dialectic of free offering, of gratitude and of free and liberating communion, advances along the way of life. To that person is revealed the clear and profound nature of things, the meaning of human life and death. In this light, too, one understands why "in the evening of life we will be judged on love" (St. John of the Cross).

This does not take place in the solitude of a spirit satiated with itself, loving self alone. The otherness that love requires is real. There is a real *you*, a real *we*. A community is a house of love. In the concreteness of daily life, it expresses the truth of the story of love. As such, a community has to be the sum of so many free origins of love. Not only one but many free offerings are required to make a common journey. Each one is an origin for the other; each one is the beginning of love; each one urgently needs to begin to love.

Every manifestation of idolatry, which refers the beginning of love to only one person, every cult of personality or blind sacrifice of diversity, spells the loss and the end of love. Each person is and must be himself or herself, loving and accepting love. For this reason, the varied and complex sum of different origins becomes communion only when each person as an origin agrees to become acceptance and arrival. One who thinks that he or she does not need others will remain in the solitude of a loveless life. One who learns from another and becomes a beggar of love makes bonds of peace and helps increase communion for everyone.

Finally, if we want the community to reflect and truly build a history of love, this interplay of giving and receiving, of free offering and gratitude, must be open. Within the secure enclosure of a clique, where love does not free hidden energies and give rise to new exoduses and new advents of love, community does not exist. Whatever love there is, withers and dies. The dialectic of diversity and communion, the original and originating interplay of love, is no less demanding for the community than it is for the individual.

b) This already tells us how difficult the effort to love is. If we survey the vast world of human relationships, the evidence of failure to love seems loud and alarming. Created to love, human beings appear incapable of loving; originating from love, they no longer seem to know how to enkindle love. To paraphrase a line from Hemingway, we could say: "The eyes that have contemplated Auschwitz and Hiroshima can no longer contemplate love."

The table of history offers the sorrowful bread of lack of love in three basic forms. These paralyze the dynamism that constitutes love. They are: jealous possession, bitter ingratitude and hurtful subjection.

Jealous possession is the opposite of free offering. In it the origin stagnates, the beginning is converted into an end. This is the attitude of a person who places self at the center of life and becomes the standard and measure of others and of all things. It is the greedy and illusory amassing of security and material things that are destined to perish. "'I shall tear down my barns and build larger ones. There I shall store all my grain and other goods and I shall say to myself, "Now, as for you, you have so many good things stored up for many years, rest, eat, drink, be merry."' But God said to him, 'You fool, this night your life will be demanded of you'" (Lk 12:18-20). Possession paralyzes love because it impedes the gift. It blocks the exodus, the emergence from self, and so it is the slave of death.

Bitter ingratitude is the opposite of the joyous acceptance of love. In it the coming of the other person is hindered and a "thank you" does not issue from the lips and the heart. When one does not let himself or herself be loved, love remains blocked; where there is no gratitude, the gift is lost. Ingratitude ignores the coming; therefore, it is bitter, sad and bored by the absence of the new and surprising.

Lastly, hurtful subjection is the opposite of the liberating communion of love. There is a beginning and an end, a starting point and an arrival, but the summit is absent, for the present moment of the lovers is closed. It is possession in the plural, reciprocal jealousy, fear of losing the moment attained, surfeit in an incompleted arrival and in an exodus only just begun. Subjection is hurtful because it separates the persons from others, eventually extinguishing in solitude the freedom and creativity of love. The language of love becomes an empty silence, a weary repetition of what was once alive and now is dead, in a vain attempt to keep alive a beginning that has become lifeless and has ended without becoming a new beginning.

Possession, ingratitude and subjection are diseases in the story of love. They render meaningless the elements of the miracle of love, the open and liberating unity of exodus and advent in a "today" that is already a foretaste of eternity, in a possession that is all ecstasy and in an ecstasy that is all possession.

c) Who can make people capable of loving? Who will free us from the jealousy of possession, from the bitterness of ingratitude and from the hurtfulness of subjection? In his book *The Prophet*, Gibran intuited the great response: "When you love, do not say: 'I have God in my heart,' but rather: 'I am in the heart of God.'"[5]

We become capable of loving when we discover that we have first been loved, enveloped and led by the tenderness of love toward a future that love builds in us and for us. To make this discovery is to believe in and profess the Trinity of the Christian God, even without words, in the truth of acts of charity, given and received.

Today theology is becoming aware that the Trinity has been too long exiled from the theory and practice of the faithful: it is making a return pilgrimage to the trinitarian, original and final homeland.[6] Studying the sacred account of the

Cross and Resurrection of the Lord, theology treasures the truth, conveyed by western iconography, which has lovingly represented the Trinity in the abandonment of the Cross, and by eastern iconography, which has instead depicted the Trinity in the angelic banquet offered by Abraham, a prefiguration of the Supper of the Risen Lord. When speaking about God, theology is again learning to speak about love.[7] It recounts the story of the love of the Father, of the Son and of the Holy Spirit among themselves and for the world, as offered in the paschal event. Theology seeks to communicate this story and help it influence the countless human stories that are marked by the effort to love.

Theology looks into the depth of the mystery and sees the eternal Spring of love in the figure of the Father, the beginning without a beginning, the pure and absolute free offering, who gives a beginning to everything in love and is not stopped even by the painful rejection of infidelity and sin.

And alongside the eternal Lover, theology tells of the Son, the eternally Beloved, the pure acceptance of Love, who teaches us that "divine" means not only giving but also receiving. His life in the flesh is an authentic "accepted existence," lived in filial obedience. He enables us to say the "yes" of faith to the initiative of God's love.

With the Lover and the Beloved, theology contemplates the figure of the Spirit, who unites both in the bond of eternal Love and opens them together to the gift of self, to the generous exodus of creation and salvation. As God's ecstasy, the Holy Spirit comes to liberate love, to make it ever new and radiant.

In the *perichoresis* of eternal love, in the unceasing dynamism of reciprocal giving and receiving, open to give being and life to his beloved creatures and to bring them into the eternal communion of the divine Persons, the Christian God offers himself as the radiant event of eternal love: "Indeed, if you see love, you see the Trinity."[8] "There are three: the Lover, the Beloved and Love."[9] "And not more than three: the One who loves him who comes from himself, the One who loves him from whom he comes, and love itself.... And if this is nothing, in what way is God love? And if this is not substance, in what way is God substance?"[10] "God is love. God is not only *in* love, as those persons who love each other are in love. God is not only I loving and you beloved. God is, rather, the radiating event of love itself."[11]

Thus it is that—through the Son's revelation and the Spirit's mission—the Trinity offers itself as the origin, womb and eternal home of love. Everything originates in the Trinity and bears its imprint: being is, in its deepest sense, love, and human beings are made to love. Everything lives in the Trinity. When the exodus of human existence opens itself to the gift that is proclaimed and bestowed, the free offering becomes new and possible in the gift of the charity of the Father; gratitude unfolds amazingly in faith, which evokes the obedience of the Son; and the freedom of communion is realized in true hope, the imprint of the Holy Spirit, which unites all ages in the eternity of love and opens them to perennial divine newness.

In this life, touched and filled by love, everything will tend toward the Trinity, the goal and eternal home of God's pilgrim people. One day everything will rest in the Trinity, when love will experience no more sunsets, and exodus and advent will meet forever. Then, "Kindness and truth shall meet; justice and peace shall kiss," and "Truth shall spring out of the earth, and justice shall look down from heaven" (Ps 85:11-12).

Being so loved by God, we can become capable of loving our neighbor: "Only a soul loved by God can accept the commandment of love of neighbor to the point of fulfilling it. God must turn to man before man can be converted to God's will."[12] Enveloped by eternal love, animated by and accepted into the trinitarian story of love, we can now build stories of love in the humble days of our lives.

Theology is "the teaching of charity," the wisdom of love, "charity seeking understanding," love that wants to be spoken and to communicate itself in words and in life. Theology will not cease to shed light and to ease the burden of loving with the story of the day of love—the day on which, in the Cross and Resurrection of the Poor One, heaven and earth met, to enable exodus and advent to encounter one another in ever new days of love.

d) As an original and originating experience, love expresses its constitutive dialectical structure in dialogue. It is in dialogue that the interplay of diversity and communion is expressed in words and actions. It could be said that the deep-rooted level of being expresses itself through communication in existential concreteness. By communicating, human beings exist fully, because they express themselves in their root vocation to love and to bring about love's realization, even if in the dynamism of a journey never fully completed.

What actual existence is to the mystery of being, dialogue is to love. As the manifestation of love, dialogue brings love's story into the humble concreteness of daily life. As an "encounter in words," dialogue is an emergence from self, an acceptance of the other, a unifying and liberating communication between both. The origin, the arrival and the summit proper to the story of love are expressed and put into language.

Dialogue is the language of love and, hence, its "dwelling," the place where love can reveal itself. Therefore, where there is no love, there can be no dialogue; but also, analogously, where there is no dialogue it is doubtful that there is any real love. We could venture to make the bold statement that where one does not communicate, one does not love and thus is not fully human. Communication is the measure of life's authenticity, of the wealth of each person's humanity.

The effort to love is invariably mirrored, therefore, in the resistance and risks proper to a life of communication. Just as the initiative of love is withered by jealous possession, which spells death to free offering, communication does not begin and does not really exist unless it is initiated and fed by a pure spring, free from any calculating and selfish interest. Nothing is more opposed to the nature of dialogue, which is a sign of the presence of charity, than strategy or tactics. When dialogue is an instrument for dominating the other person or manipulating him or her for one's own ends, it simply ceases to exist.

We can say that dialogue, like love, has the dignity of an end and not of a means. It reveals a free offering and proposes itself as an offer of encounter that springs from the pure joy of loving. This implies that the initiative should be joined to the acceptance of the other person, in all the substance of his or her diversity. Just as love does not live without grateful acceptance, so dialogue is not born and does not develop where the dignity and character of the other person are not respected. Monologue, which simply ignores the needs and gifts of the other person, frustrates the encounter, making it purely incidental. Dialogue, on the contrary, needs for its existence a "reciprocity of awareness" (M. Nedoncelle), a fruitful exchange in which giving and receiving are measured solely by free offering and humble and true acceptance on the part of each of the two persons.[13]

To ignore others' individuality is to exclude any possibility of dialogue. The recognition of diversity as a gift to be accepted, and not as a risk to be warded off, is essential to dialogue. For love to be true, however, initiative and acceptance must not remain closed within a circle of two persons. Likewise, freedom from every form of possessiveness is necessary for the possibility and effective realization of dialogue. Where there is dependence or clannishness, dialogue declines. It is authentic not only when it is born in an atmosphere of freedom, but when it presents itself as a liberating experience, constantly open to others, inclusive and never exclusive of their needs and deep concerns.

An "encounter in words" must make other encounters possible. It reaches outside the circle of the two persons, toward the vast world of solidarity and companionship. It is here that we understand how dialogue and mission do not oppose one another but are to be, in a certain sense, each other's strength and authenticity.

What is freely given and received in the dialogue of charity must still be freely offered through new avenues of communication. In dialogue, the hidden energies of love are unshackled, and one's existence, far from inauthentically closing in on itself, projects itself outward, becoming both service and gift. This opening outward does not stifle the communion of those engaged in dialogue; rather, it makes their communication true and joyful.

The effort to love, therefore, is the endeavor to dialogue. It can be sustained and can lead to a truly communicative existence only if we recognize that we were first called by Another in the dialogue of love. "There is no greater invitation to love than to take the first step in loving."[14] For Christian faith, it is in the revelation of the mystery of a Triune God, who "loved them to the end" (Jn 13:1), that we can realize that we were first loved, enfolded and inserted, as it were, into the eternal communication of divine charity.

Faith in the communicating Trinity, the God who is Love, is the most fundamental theological basis for an ecclesial lifestyle inspired and shaped by dialogue. Through dialogue, we respond to the First Love, in the Spirit who has been given to us; through dialogue, we bear witness to others that we have believed in love: "This is how all will know that you are my disciples, if you have love for one another" (Jn 13:35).

Without dialogue among its members, the Church will never be the "Icon of the Trinity," the humble and meaningful reflection in time of the eternal communion of the Triune God. Without a dialogue of concern and friendship with the community of humankind, the Church will not proclaim the Good News that has been freely revealed and given to it by Christ. If communication is the sign of the presence of love, and if it is on love that we shall be judged, we could say that dialogue is the measure of the authenticity of ecclesial life and of the missionary commitment of believers.

In this light, too, ecumenism—which is the "dialogue of charity" become an ecclesial lifestyle—appears as an urgent need for those who believe in the Gospel of love. A theology of communication as a theology of love lays the groundwork for a Christian and ecclesial activity that is born of dialogue, lives of dialogue and is on the march toward the eternal communion of "God, who is all in all" (cf 1 Cor 15:28).

Part Two

Eucharist

Introduction

"If you are the body and the members of Christ, your mystery is placed on the table of the Lord: you receive your own mystery! You respond 'Amen' to that which you are, and with your reply you assent. You hear it said, 'Body of Christ!' and you respond, 'Amen!' Be, therefore, members of the Body of Christ that your 'Amen' may be true."[1] These words, addressed by the Bishop of Hippo to all who were receiving Communion for the first time, were intended to shed light on the most profound meaning of their action. St. Augustine highlights the unbreakable bond that exists between the Eucharist and the Church. The first millennium used the same expression, without any difference, for both realities: Body of Christ.

It was only later—between the ninth and eleventh centuries—when the rationalistic interpretations of the "new" logic of dialectics aimed at denying the truth of the Eucharistic Body of the Lord, that it was felt necessary to add the adjective "mystical" to the expression "Body of Christ" in speaking of the Church. The "true Body of Christ," which is the Eucharist, was contrasted with the "mystical Body of Christ," which is the Church. The separation thus introduced into the mystery was to be reflected in ecclesiological concepts that more and more stressed the visible and juridical aspects of the ecclesial reality and at the same time obscured the nourishing, vigorous and ever new presence of the Spirit in the Church. Thus it was that in the West there spread that vision which Yves Congar characterized as "christomonism." This term refers to the preferential attention given to the "incarnationist" aspects of the Church, and therefore to the visible and organic dimension of the universal unity of all baptized persons. The Church would be considered in the guise of the "Serene Republic of Venice" (Robert Bellarmine), as a self-sufficient historical institution (a "perfect society"), with its own laws, its own rites and its own leaders, firmly brought back into the scheme of worldly "wisdom."

The Second Vatican Council marked a decisive development in the history of Christian events, especially because it rediscovered the trinitarian origin of the Church, and therefore the impossibility of reducing the latter to a purely secular understanding and appraisal. The Church comes from the Trinity, reflects in itself the trinitarian communion—oneness in diversity—and journeys toward the Trinity, to the final handing over of all things to Christ, so that he might hand them over to the Father and God might be all in all. As "a people gathered in the unity of the Father and of the Son and of the Holy Spirit,"[2] the Church is the Church of the Father. In his universal salvific plan, God has willed it to be a sign and instrument of the unity of people among themselves and with him. It is the Church of the Son, who through his incarnation and the paschal mystery has placed it in history as his Body. It is the Church of the Spirit, who makes the Risen Christ present in human history and, enriching the people of God with charisms and ministries, leads it toward the promised future goal.

The Church is therefore between times: between the time of its origins, which belong to the Father and are fulfilled in history in the sending of the Son and of the Holy Spirit, and the end of time, which is the glory of God in all things.

The Church is the meeting place of trinitarian history and human history, where the former continually enters into the latter to transform and vitalize it, and where the change and growth of this world are brought to their fulfillment in God. The Church is the sign of the divine presence among human persons, of the Trinity in time, of the glory already hidden in history: it is the "Kingdom of God present in mystery."[3]

This status as a place of alliance ("ark of the

covenant") demands that the Church be concretely situated in the world of humankind. The initiative and fidelity of the Trinity, who raises up the ecclesial community, are not addressed to a non-existent, abstract history, but to concrete histories. It is into them that the movement of the Spirit enters, flowing from the Father through the Son and always in the act of returning through the Son to the Father. It is the Spirit who makes the Trinity present here and now, and it is in the Spirit that every fragment of time and space has access to the trinitarian mystery of the beginning. The Spirit assures us how seriously the God of Christians takes human history and makes it his own. The historical dimension of the mystery is the Spirit; he gives it to the Church. Now the action of the Spirit, the source of communion within the time and space of a concrete historical situation, does not take place invisibly, outside of or contrary to the logic of the Incarnation. If we must not separate Christ from the Spirit (christomonism), neither are we to separate the Spirit from Christ (as may happen in some forms of the Pentecostal renewal). The event of the Spirit never prescinds from the Christ-event; it is, rather, the representation of that event, its realization in the variety of human events. The privileged places for the outpouring of the Spirit are, therefore, those which Christ entrusted to his followers, that is, the Word and the living signs of the New

Covenant. The event which sums up all of them and which is considered the "culmination and source" of them all, is the celebration of the Eucharist. In it is fulfilled the "memorial" of the Pasch of the Lord; in it, through the Word and the Spirit, Christ who died and was raised up by the Father is made present to reconcile human beings with God and among themselves. A renewed understanding of the trinitarian depth of the Church and a rediscovery of the eucharistic ecclesiology proper to the first millennium thus converge.

Like the Church, the Eucharist is totally related to the Trinity. It is the great act of thanksgiving to the Father for all that he has accomplished, does accomplish and will accomplish for the human family. It is a sacrifice of praise in which the whole of creation is offered to become a kingdom of justice, love and peace. It is the memorial of Christ crucified and risen, that is, the living and effective sign of his unique and unrepeatable sacrifice, which becomes present to reconcile people with God today. It is the invocation of the Holy Spirit, in which praise rises to the Father and in which there comes from the Father the gift of the life-giving presence of the Risen One.[4]

In the Eucharist trinitarian history and human history meet, the covenant is celebrated, the Church of the Trinity is born and expresses itself.

In the Eucharist the opposite temptations—of a Church solely visible and juridical and of a Church invisible and out of reach (christomonism and pneumatomonism)—are taken up and overcome. The Eucharist is an event of the Spirit and is at the same time an institution of Christ, faithfully transmitted by the Church. It is charismatic newness and at the same time continuity in the "tradition of the Church," structured ministerially. It is the "now" entrusted by the Lord and at the same time the pledge of the "not yet" of his promise. In this twofold sense—pneumatological and christological, beginning from the Spirit and beginning from Christ—both of these statements are true: the Eucharist makes the Church and the Church makes the Eucharist. The Eucharist makes the Church in that it is the place of the action of the Spirit, who re-presents the Passover of the Lord and thus gathers people together in the reconciliation it effects. The Church makes the Eucharist in that it is the celebrating community which, in obedience to the command of Christ, is joined in its ministerial form to celebrate the "memorial" of the New Covenant.

Therefore, the Christian faith recognizes in the Eucharist the "sacrament of unity" and can use the same term to designate both the Eucharist and the Church: Corpus Christi, the Body of Christ. Thus, too, the renewal of the Church, understood as the overcoming of every type of juridical reductionism and spiritualizing alienation, cannot but experience a rediscovery of the Eucharist at the center of the Christian community and of its mission.

It is with attentiveness to this renewal and this rediscovery that the following pages unfold. Prepared as lectures,[5] they aim to present in a brief and concise manner the fundamental features of the relationship between the Eucharist and ecclesial communion and the Eucharist and mission. Referring back, for a broader ecclesiological context and for documentation, to my book, *La chiesa nell'eucaristia: per un'ecclesiologia eucaristica alla luce del Vaticano II*,[6] these two chapters propose to offer an active and immediate contribution to the intense work of deeper study being carried out in these years on the theme of the Eucharist and the Church.

3. Eucharist and Communion

If in Jesus Christ "heaven has come down to earth and has taken root there" (Hegel), living as his follower means inevitably belonging to two worlds and celebrating in one's own person the encounter of two fidelities: fidelity to heaven and fidelity to earth, nostalgia for the "homeland" and love for the "alien land." United with all people in the companionship of life, Christians are both a pilgrim people journeying toward the promised land and a people in exodus, continually called to "go to him [Jesus Christ] outside the camp, bearing the reproach that he bore. For here we have no lasting city, but we seek one that is to come" (Heb 13:13-14). This people's duty is to keep alive the watchful and steadfast expectation of those new things to come. It is to sing in the midst of humankind the deeds of the Most High, notwithstanding the weight of the present cross, which causes one to weep in the night of exile: "How could we sing a song of the LORD in a

foreign land?" (Ps 137:4). Balanced between the
gift "already" received and the restlessness of the
promise "not yet" fulfilled, the Church continually discovers anew its condition as communion
of life that comes "from on high," constituted in
the image of the Trinity through the action of the
Spirit, and which journeys toward the heights,
toward the homeland which is with the Father.

The place of this ever new "discovery" is the
celebration of the Eucharist. In it the Church celebrates entirely the "memorial" of its origin and
of its promised end. This "memorial" is not to be
understood in the weak sense of the western concept, by which it would signify movement from
the present to the past through a kind of uplift-
ing of the spirit; this, rather, in exactly the opposite sense, is the biblical "memorial" (*anamnesis,
mnemosunon, zikkaron, azkarah*), indicating a movement that reaches from the past into the present
and thanks to which, in the power of the divine
Spirit, the unique and definitive salvific event is
made present, living and effective for the celebrating community.

In the eucharistic memorial the events of the
paschal mystery are not only remembered, but—
in and through this memorial celebration—are
made present and real, so that, without losing
anything of their unrepeatable uniqueness, they
reach into the concrete moment and fill it with
their power, making it a time of grace, an hour of

salvation for those who receive the gift in the gratitude of faith. At the same time, the memory of the original salvific event is charged with the promise contained in it: the memorial of the paschal mystery is at the same time a memorial of the "homeland," a memory that anticipates the future goal, always glimpsed and never fully possessed. Thus it happens that in the eucharistic memorial celebration the Church is brought forth and expressed and grows toward its fulfillment. The Eucharist builds up the Church into the Body of Christ, because it is, in the Spirit, the living memory of its origin, the memorial of its present and the anticipatory memory of its coming.

The Eucharistic Remembrance of the Beginning: The Church as Mystery, Gift and Pledge

The love of the Trinity precedes the love of humanity. The Church is not the fruit of "flesh and blood"; it is not a flower sprouting out of the earth. It is a gift from on high, a fruit of the divine initiative. Ever a part of the Father's saving plan, it was prepared by him in the history of the covenant with Israel, so that when the time was fulfilled, it was born in the outpouring of the Spirit.[1] Like its Lord, the Church is the "dawn from on high": its origin is not here below, in a convergence of human interests or in the impulse of a generous heart. Its origin is "on high," with

God, whence came the Son in the flesh, to bring this flesh to life in the power—at once mortal and transforming—of the trinitarian life.

With the history of Easter, the Spirit entered in a full and definitive manner into the affairs of this world. God had "time for man" (Karl Barth), and beginning from the dawn of the resurrection, the days of humankind became the "penultimate" time, that is, the time between the first coming of the Son of man and his return in glory—a time of the Spirit, who now works ceaselessly in human affairs. The self-emptying of the Word into shadowy human flesh was followed, according to a very rich image of the Eastern Fathers, by the self-emptying of the Spirit into the shadowy Spouse: from the mission of the Son and of the Spirit the Church was born!

This action of the trinitarian history of God in the history of the world, which promoted a new communion among peoples, is rendered present in a way that is at once a culmination and a source, in the event of the Eucharist. In it the Church is gathered to celebrate the "memory" of its origin in the paschal mystery of Christ, to prepare itself to welcome and praise the action of the Father, who sends the Holy Spirit and makes the crucified and risen Christ present among his people. The community that gathers to celebrate the eucharistic memorial is actually a sign of the divine initiative breaking into the present moment and bringing to life the events of salvation, which were accomplished in a unique and definitive way in the paschal history of Jesus of Nazareth. In the same act in which the Church makes the Eucharist, it is in reality the Eucharist that makes the Church, in its threefold condition of "mystery," gift and pledge.

In the first place, the eucharistic memorial of the beginning forms the Church in its reality as "mystery." As the fruit of the initiative of the Trinity, the eucharistic Church, in its most profound nature, is inaccessible to purely human understanding; it is the "mystical" Body (that is, the Body "in mystery") of Christ. According to the Pauline biblical concept, "mystery" is the divine plan of salvation that is being carried out in history without, however, letting itself be trapped within the limits of this world. Even if it is true (and it must never be disregarded) that the Church is a presence among other presences in history, it is also true that it is the place of another Presence, a living memory of One who, having entered into history, did not let himself be reduced to history. Born in the Easter memorial, the Church has its origin elsewhere. Those who want to measure and define the Church according to the analogies of this world, those who want to see it as nothing more than a power among other powers in the course of human events, will never know the heart of the Church.

"Blessed are those invited to the Lord's supper": for those who respond to this invitation, another world appears in our world, the Spirit enters the flesh, kills it and raises it up to a new, unimaginable life.

This meeting place between worlds, this strange though familiar land, this intersecting of a familiar plane by another that is unfamiliar and powerful, is the Eucharistic Mystery, from which is born the "mystery" of the Church, the "tent" of God among humankind, the particle of flesh and of time in which the Spirit of the Eternal has made his dwelling. Those who in speaking of the Church would neglect this dimension of its origin and source, those who would describe in great detail the Church's internal structure and its past relationships with the forces at work in history while forgetting to recognize the fullness of its eucharistic origin (thereby ignoring the other plane, because it is unknown and unlooked for), would certainly be thinking "according to men," but not "according to God."

This is why the Second Vatican Council's reflection on the Church opens with a chapter that can be considered the key for reading everything that follows: "On the Mystery of the Church." The Church is a mystery! In the heart of this chapter, one text recalls the eucharistic memorial of the beginning, from which the Church is born and by which it is expressed: "As often as the sacrifice of the cross in which Christ our Passover was sacrificed (1 Cor 5:7) is celebrated on the altar, the work of our redemption is carried on, and, in the sacrament of the eucharistic bread, the unity of all believers who form one Body in Christ (cf 1 Cor 10:17) is both expressed and brought about. Everyone is called to this union with Christ, who is the light of the world, from whom we go forth, through whom we live, and toward whom our whole life strains."[2] As the divine plan of salvation accomplished in history, the "mystery" is offered and expressed in the most profound manner in the eucharistic event, the memorial of the Cross and Resurrection of Christ, our Passover, the constitutive source of his ecclesial Body!

In the second place, the eucharistic memorial of the beginning sheds light on the Church as "gift." As the Body given by the Lord, the Church is not invented or produced, but received. It is not the fruit of human effort, but is the free and gratuitous offering of a grace, which neither is nor can be merited. The eucharistic Church is born from the reception of this grace and from thanksgiving for it: "Father, all-powerful and ever-living God, we do well always and everywhere to give you thanks through Jesus Christ our Lord...." Where the Father is adored in persevering expectation, where thanksgiving is celebrated in the powerful memorial that renews the presence of the crucified and risen Christ among his people—there the Spirit rushes in. Now challenging, now consoling, the Spirit raises up the family of God's children: hence, the Church's need for a contemplative and eucharistic style of life.

The memory of the beginning, lived in the Eucharist, teaches that it is not the wealth of human means that builds up the Church. Rather, it is not in spite of but precisely through the lack of human means that the Church is built up! Just as "the pierced hands of Jesus on the cross accomplished more for the glory of God and our salvation than those same hands did when they commanded the wind and the sea," so the hands raised toward heaven by a people especially capable of praise and thanksgiving will do more for the coming of the Kingdom than those same hands engaged in a task that has no soul. In the Church, the primacy in being, as in working, belongs to God: to him alone do we give the glory, from him alone do we await salvation. "The Eucharist belongs to the economy of grace, which unfolds through time and space. It enters into the dialogical structure of a covenant whose very initiative belongs to God."[3] Born from the Eucharist, the Church is therefore faithfully represented in Mary, its model and ideal, whose virginal motherhood is the sign of the pure welcome and pure grace with which God intervenes in the history of humankind.

In the third place, the eucharistic memorial of the beginning brings into relief the historical commitment of the Church, the Body of Christ given for the multitudes. Just as the Word became flesh, entering into the very depths of the contradiction of human existence and even into death; just as in the eucharistic event the Crucified and Risen One is present to all human situations, to permeate them with his power of reconciliation and life; so the Church, born of the eucharistic Pasch, must make itself present to all human suffering, to the hunger for justice and freedom, in order to convey the transforming power of the Redeemer of humankind.

The contemplative and eucharistic character of the Church's being and acting cannot signify a flight from the world or fear of being involved in it. If the God of the Church became totally part of human events, the Church cannot remain a spectator of history. The glory of God is celebrated where human life is promoted: "the glory of God is man fully alive" (St. Irenaeus of Lyons). There is no human situation, especially that of suffering and misery, that cannot be brought to the eucharistic memorial of Passover liberation, and therefore there is no human situation from which the Church can feel estranged. Its duty is to be present in a fellowship of which the eucharistic banquet around the one Bread is sign and source.

The powerful memory of reconciliation generates a Church that journeys with humankind. Living in the companionship of life, it is able to bring to the Father its tears and protests and at the same time to prophetically announce to all people the other dimension, the horizon of the Kingdom which is coming, a protest against and an overturning of the nearsightedness of this world's calculations and conceit. It is a Church whose solidarity proclaims joy and hope—a joy and hope that come to it from the "yes" spoken to humankind by God in Jesus Christ. At the same time, it is a Church free from and opposed to the compromises of the "power mentality" of this present age, a Church that is a witness of the "no" with which, in the Cross of Christ, God has judged all crucifiers throughout history. A poor servant, the voice of humankind speaking to God and the voice of God speaking to humankind in the reality of history: this is the condition of the eucharistic Church, born "from on high" in the effective memorial of its paschal origin, continually raised up anew by the Spirit in the flesh and blood of this world.

The Eucharistic Memorial of the Present: The Church as "Communion of Saints"

Coming from on high, the Church is brought forth and expressed by the eucharistic memorial in the "now" of history as a communion of life in the Spirit. Reconciled with God and with each other in Christ through the sacramental representation of the paschal event, the faithful constitute one Body in him. Common participation in the same Bread forms the unity of the ecclesial Body, because that unique Bread is the sacrament of Christ who died and is glorified as the Reconciler. "Really partaking of the body of the Lord in the breaking of the eucharistic bread, we are taken up into communion with him and with one another. 'Because the bread is one, we though many, are one body, all of us who partake of the one bread' (1 Cor 10:17). In this way all of us are made members of his Body (cf 1 Cor 12:17), 'but severally members one of another' (Rom 12:5)."[4] The Eucharist, the memorial of the paschal origin of the Church, is therefore also the effective memorial of the Church's present. It is an event in which, between the time of the beginning and the time of the final days, the communion of life in Christ is born today and is expressed in the community of the pilgrim people.

An ancient expression of faith that is rich in meaning conveys this eucharistic nature of the Church "between times." This expression is contained in the most ancient creeds, where it is mentioned after the Holy Spirit and the holy catholic Church: "the communion of saints." This "brief and tremendous" expression embraces three meanings or levels of depth. In the very arrangement of the terms (Spirit, Church, communion of saints) these levels can be used to characterize the Church, formed in its present reality by the eucharistic memorial. The first meaning touches the most profound level of this "ecclesial memorial": the Church is a "communion of the Holy" *(communio Sancti),* a communion in the Spirit of Christ. In the second place, "communion of the holy" *(communio sanctorum)* means the communion of the sacramental realities through which we receive the Spirit. Finally, in the meaning of the personal genitive plural, the expression refers to the communion of saints, the community of men and women reborn in the Spirit for eternal life.

Born in the present through the eucharistic memorial, the Church is above all a "communion of the Holy," a community of the Spirit of Christ, "spiritual Body" (that is, *in the Holy Spirit).* It is the place of the unheard-of encounter between the world of the Spirit and the world of human beings. Therefore, totally immersed in the history, sufferings and sorrows of human life, the Church is called to bring to all people the proclamation and the gift of the new world of God, revealed in Jesus Christ. In every time and in every situation, it brings about the encounter between the Spirit and the flesh, between God and humankind, which is realized in Christ.

Christ Jesus is the One who has received and given the Spirit. He received the Spirit in his condition of humiliation, from his conception to his baptism, from his ministry to his sacrifice; he received the Spirit in his supreme self-emptying on the cross. His resurrection is truly the great trinitarian event in which the Father through the action of the Spirit gives new and glorious life to the Incarnate Son who died for us. The gift of the Spirit raised the Crucified One. The Risen Christ is therefore filled with the Spirit, and can pour out this abundance on every person. Having received the Spirit, Christ gives him: "And when I am lifted up from the earth, I will draw everyone to myself" (John 12:32). "Receive the holy Spirit" (John 20:22).

Compared "by no weak analogy" to the mystery of the Incarnate Word,[5] the Church, too, receives and gives the Spirit: it is the gift of the Spirit that raises up the Church. "The Spirit dwells in the Church and in the hearts of the faithful, as in a temple. In them he prays on their behalf and bears witness to the fact that they are adopted children. The Church, which the Spirit guides in the way of all truth and which he unified in communion and in works of ministry, he both equips and directs with hierarchical and charismatic gifts and adorns with his fruits. By the power of the Gospel he makes the Church keep the freshness of youth. Uninterruptedly he renews it and leads it to perfect union with its Spouse."[6]

Springing up from the eucharistic memorial,

the Church is the Temple of the Spirit, the Body of Christ, the "people gathered together by the unity of the Father, of the Son and of the Holy Spirit."[7] Just as it receives the Spirit through Christ from the Father, so the Church is called to give the Spirit. Its mission is summarized in the mandate to bring the entire universe to the Father through Christ in the Holy Spirit. It is the sign and instrument, or rather the sacrament, through which the Spirit brings about the unity of human beings with God and among themselves.

The eucharistic Church receives the Spirit: it is the place of the outpouring of God's gift in time. Like Mary, it is continually and in an ever new way overshadowed by the Spirit, in order to conceive the divine Word in history. Brought forth in the womb of Mother Church, Christian life is life according to the Spirit. "For those who are led by the Spirit of God are children of God" (Rom 8:14). Christians are anointed by the Spirit: in baptism and in the sacramental economy they are configured with Christ, and through him and in him are filled with the Holy Spirit. Here is the profound reason for Christian "newness," for the difference, that is, between being Christian and entering history on a purely natural level. Here too lie the source and beginning of every specific gift and service. Here are rooted both the unity and diversity of the Church, communion and forms of ministry.

The eucharistic Church is the "communion of saints" *(communio sanctorum fidelium),* in the sense that the baptized share in the one Spirit and are enriched by the variety of his gifts. The Spirit unceasingly distributes these gifts to each one as he wills. They are called "charisms," that is, gifts freely bestowed, the fruit of the freedom and creativity of the Spirit, lavished by him with overflowing richness, and directed to the growth of the entire Body of Christ. "To each individual the manifestation of the Spirit is given for the common good" (cf 1 Cor 12:7). Every Christian is a "charismatic," if he or she recognizes and accepts the gift of God. The imagination of the Spirit is inexhaustible and his work untiring. No baptized person has the right to excuse himself or herself from the baptismal commitment, because each one is endowed with charisms to live in service and communion. No one has the right to division or separation, because the charisms come from the one Lord and are directed to the building up of the one Body, which is the Church (cf 1 Cor 12:4-7). No one has the right to stand still or to long for the past, because the Spirit is always living and active. He is the newness of God, he is the Lord of the future.

The eucharistic Church gives the Spirit: it is the privileged sign and instrument in the history of the Spirit's activity. It is the sacrament of Christ, just as Christ is the sacrament of the Father. It is his living and life-giving Body. This total sacramentality of the Church is expressed in two privileged ways: the Word of God, which by challenging and enlightening calls people to salvation, and the Sacrament, the highest Presence of the Word, the re-presentation of the paschal mystery of Christ in the life of humankind. Word and Sacrament are eminently present and converge in the Eucharistic Celebration. As the memorial of the Passover of Christ, that is, the re-actualization of it, in different times and places, the Eucharist reconciles humankind with God and among themselves. It is the "sacrament of unity," the one Bread from which is born the one Body of Christ, which is the Church, through the action of the Spirit. In the Eucharist, Word and Bread are the sacrament from which ecclesial communion springs. The Eucharist forms the Church, the communion of the holy realities given in the eucharistic memorial *(communio sanctorum sacramentorum)*.

The eucharistic Church is above all the local church, an assembly celebrating in a definite space and time. But this local church is the Church in its fullness, Catholic in the etymological sense *(katholou* = in fullness), because it is one and holy in the unique Body of the Eucharistic Christ and in the one Spirit, and apostolic in its fidelity to the mandate entrusted by Jesus to the apostles and to their successors: "Do this in memory of me." The same Christ and the same Spirit, then, establish the communion of each local church with the others, the universal communion of the churches, born from the same Word, the same Bread, the same Spirit. Every local church recognizes itself in every other eucharistic Church, because it recognizes the one Lord of all the churches present in his Spirit.

If the Eucharist forms the Church, it is also true that the Church makes the Eucharist. The Word is not proclaimed if there is no one to announce it; the memorial is not celebrated if there is no one to do it in obedience to the Lord's mandate. Word and Sacrament, therefore, require the ministry of the Church, the service of proclamation, of the celebration of the sacrifice, and of the regathering of the scattered human family into the unity of the holy people of God. The eucharistic Church is totally ministerial: totally committed to this threefold role: prophetic, priestly and royal.[8] Every baptized person is formed by the Spirit into the likeness of Christ, Priest, Prophet and King, and consequently, in communion with all the others, committed to proclaiming the Word of God with his or her life, to celebrating the Easter memorial in order to bring about in history the justice of the coming Kingdom of God.

The Eucharistic Memorial of the Final Days:
The Poor, Servant Church, a People Rejoicing

"Amen, I say to you, I shall not drink again the fruit of the vine until that day when I drink it new in the kingdom of God" (Mk 14:25). The Eucharistic Supper, entrusted by Jesus to his followers as a memorial of his Passover, is a sign and foretaste of the future glory that will be fully revealed when Christ returns to inaugurate the final Banquet of the Kingdom. The Eucharist is both the remembrance of the origin of the ecclesial community and the "anticipatory remembrance" of its future destiny. It reminds the people of God that they are a people in exodus, a pilgrim people journeying toward the promised homeland. In the Spirit and through Christ, the Church proceeds toward the Father. It continually reaches upward toward the heights, toward the glory of the Lord of heaven and earth, who is also the full realization of his creatures.

Ever born anew in the eucharistic memorial of the events of salvation, the Church is driven by these events to be always open to the future. The gift "already" received is a foretaste and promise of the greatest gift, "not yet" attained. It is a gift that does not satisfy our expectation, but challenges and changes it, making it more alive and consuming. It is a sign of the homeland that is glimpsed but not yet possessed, the rejection of every type of idolatry in the present age in view of openness to realities that are new or coming into being.

"Sacrament of the future," the Eucharist bears witness to the promised future that enlightens the quality of the Church's life and action as the very dimension that reaches out to everything and gives life and offers the horizon of the final days that gives meaning and value to every step of the unending journey. Three consequences stem from this for the existence of the Church, born of the Eucharist.

In the first place, the eucharistic memorial of the promised end reminds the Church of its radical poverty, of its condition as the Body of Christ crucified in history. Faced with the future of the Lord who is coming, the Church is aware of its dependency; it discovers it is not an absolute, but an instrument, not an end but a means, a poor and pilgrim people. Viaticum, the Bread of travelers journeying toward the promised land, nourishes the people of God so it will know how to wait in fidelity, like the aging Simeon, until night passes and light dawns to illumine the people forever. No attainment, no success should temper the eucharistic community's ardor of expectation. Each "ecstasy of achievement" is seen as an evasion and a betrayal. Anyone who presumes to have arrived, to have achieved the goal, is challenged. The Church is "always reforming," called to continual purification and to unceasing renewal, unsatisfied and incapable of being satisfied with any human conquest. Fidelity to its past as source, the wealth of faith received through the uninterrupted living Tradition, must never be exchanged for the presumption of possession or the fear of what is new.

The eucharistic event, in which the Church, heir and transmitter of the Faith, gathers to celebrate the powerful memory of its origins and of its future goal, shows how the institution—the guardian and witness of the "now"—is constantly given new life by the outpouring of the Holy Spirit and by its openness to the "not yet" of the promise. Tradition and event, institution and charism, meet in the Easter memorial, where the Church is found and is pointed out to humankind, the Church, balanced between past and present, rich only in its poverty, welcoming the ancient and ever new gift of its God. The Church thus understands that it does not "possess" the truth, but it is "possessed" by it. In the wonder of the divine mystery that possesses it, the Church comprehends that it must allow itself to be possessed ever more by its Spouse.

Nothing is further from the style of a Church that celebrates "the memory of the future" than an attitude of triumphalism, of yielding to the dazzling seduction of power and possession in this world. The Church was born at the foot of the cross and is a pilgrim in this long Good Friday which is the history of humankind. It is ever reborn in the eucharistic re-actualization of its origin and of the anticipation of its future; therefore, it must never exchange the dim lights of earthly honor for the light promised it at Easter. Contrary to worldly logic, the finality of the eucharistic Church is to disappear, when the Kingdom, only present in the Church as a beginning, will appear in glory.

In the second place the eucharistic memorial of the coming of God teaches the Church how to put into perspective the greatness of this world, to be a vigilant servant in submitting everything to the judgment of the cross and of the resurrection of its Lord. As the Body of the crucified Christ in history, it is the Body that crucifies all the shortsightedness of history. In virtue of its loftiest goal, the eucharistic community should be critical of and overturn the shortsighted realities of this world. As it is present to every human situation, in solidarity with the poor and oppressed, it would not be right to identify its hope with any earthly hopes. Understood correctly, this does not signify cheap criticism or release from commitment. The vigilance that is asked of the Church is much more costly and demanding. It means simultaneously to take up human hopes and to verify them in light of the Resurrection. The Resurrection, on the one hand, sustains the authentic commitment to the freedom of human-kind; on the other, it opposes the absolutizing of earthly goals.

In this twofold sense, the hope of the Church, the hope of the resurrection, nourished by the "Bread of hope," the pledge of future glory, is the resurrection of hope. It gives life to whomever is a prisoner of death and shatters whatever tries to make itself an idol of life. Herein lies the profound inspiration of the Christian presence in the different cultural, political and social contexts. Because of its "eschatological reserve," which is the future promise of which the Eucharist is a pledge and foretaste, the Church cannot be identified with any ideology, with any party power, with any system, but for all of them it must be a critical conscience, a reminder of the origin and the final end, a stimulus, so that in everything the aim is the development of the whole person in everyone. The Church must be an "uncomfortable" and "disquieting" Church, free and of service, not the Church of the system, of compromise or of apparent noninvolvement; there could be a temptation to build up this kind of Church.

The "homeland" anticipated and promised in the eucharistic memorial makes us strangers and pilgrims in this world but does not alienate us from reality. Rather, it is a stimulating and critical force for commitment to justice and peace in the present situation of the world.

Finally, the eucharistic memorial of the goal fills the Church with joy. The Church is a people rejoicing, who already exult in the hope enkindled by the promise. It is the festive Body of Christ, not only his crucified and crucifying Body. In the eucharistic event and in the life that arises from it, the Church discovers that it is an active anticipation of what was promised in the resurrection of the humiliated One. There is no defeat, no victory of death, that can extinguish in the community of believers the strength of hope, always newly bestowed by the eucharistic "feast." There the last word of life and of history is guaranteed as a word of joy and not of sorrow, of grace and not of sin, of life and not of death. As the pilgrims of Zion, Christians are continually directed toward the goal that is glimpsed even if it is not yet possessed: "I rejoiced because they said to me, 'We will go up to the house of the LORD!'" (Ps 122:1). Their joy does not spring from the presumption of building with their own hands a stairway toward heaven, a kind of new tower of Babel that is a self-imprisoned world. They respond to the invitation of God, and they experience, beginning from the eucharistic event, that God has time for human persons and builds his house together with them.

"The celebration of the Eucharist is entrusted to the Church as a prophetic act which communicates to the Church the presence among us of the

new world, which began with the death and resurrection of Christ and which makes us witnesses
of it. There the Church is invited to hope: with
Christ it participates in the genesis of a humanity
that is saved and reunited, in expectation of the
day when 'God will be all in all.'"[9]

In the celebration of the eucharistic memorial,
the longed-for and awaited Jerusalem has already
come down from heaven. Believers have the task
of living the mystery of Advent in the heart of
human events. The hour of trial will come, as
well as the apparent triumph of death, but the
Church knows that, beneath the shadows of the
present, as beneath the veil of the eucharistic
signs, Christ is living and active. It is he who has
conquered the world; it is he, present in the gift
of his Supper, who is the indestructible source of
the Church's joy. The Church longs for him every time it gathers to give thanks. And to the
Church he responds with his presence and his
promise: "Yes, I am coming soon" (Rv 22:20).

4. Eucharist and Mission

There is a moment in the life of the Lord which, because of its intensity, is placed as the link between Christ in the flesh and Christ mystically prolonged in time: this key moment is the Last Supper. For Jesus it was certainly a culminating point, longed for and awaited by him at length (Lk 22:15), the supreme (Jn 13:1) and definitive "hour" (Lk 22:16, 18) of his earthly existence. Beyond that Supper there is nothing other than the fulfillment of what it foretells and illumines beforehand: the paschal mystery of death and resurrection. Therefore truly "the problem of the Last Supper is the problem of the life of Jesus" (A. Schweitzer).

What is more, as a supreme event in the life of Christ, the Supper holds an analogous importance for the life of the Church. As the threshold between the physical Christ and the Christ mystically present in time, it is the seal of the love of the former and the source of life of the latter. During the Last Supper, Jesus, in instituting the

Eucharist, instituted the Church: it was not by chance that he chose the Passover as the setting for his gift. In that way he clearly expressed his intention of substituting for the paschal memorial of the covenant that was the origin of ancient Israel, the memorial of the new covenant in his blood, the origin of the new Israel, the Church.[1] We may add that the references made to the Old Testament in the accounts of the institution of the Eucharist are all related to the idea of alliance. The reference to the blood of the covenant, which recalls Exodus 24:8; the theme of the new covenant, taken up by Jeremiah 31:31; and the numerous references to the Suffering Servant songs in Isaiah, concur in presenting the Eucharist as the memorial of the covenant of a new people.[2] The Last Supper is therefore the act of institution of the Church, in which can be found the fundamental characteristics and tasks which the Lord gave to his community.

As the culmination of the life of Jesus and source of the life of the Church, the Last Supper is thus situated as the event which sums up in itself the relationship between Christ and his people. As a consequence, even the relationship between Christ the evangelizer and the evangelizing Church can be understood in the framework of the new paschal banquet. This will be done according to an historical-biblical manner of proceeding, which guarantees both faithful-

ness to the Word of God and fruitfulness for the
history of humankind.[3]

To Evangelize Means to Celebrate in
History: The Memorial of the Lord
in the Power of the Spirit

The mission that the Lord entrusts to his Church
is totally summed up in the words he pronounced
at the Last Supper: "Do this in memory of me."
With these words, made explicit in the text of
Luke 22:19 and of 1 Corinthians 11:24-25, Jesus
entrusted to the apostles the mandate to celebrate
in history the memorial of his paschal mystery.
Matthew and Mark, who address Christians from
a Jewish background, do not feel the need to
make it so explicit, since for the Hebrew the idea
of memorial was immediately connected with that
of paschal celebration. Despite the silence of these
two gospel writers, there is a fundamental conso-
nance among the texts of the institution in grasp-
ing that what Jesus did at the Last Supper was an
event to be memorialized. And since at the Last
Supper the history of Christ reaches its climax
and at the same time everything that forms the
essential structure of the Church is present, in
this role of celebrating the eucharistic memorial
the whole mission of the Christian community in
time is truly defined.

The Church must celebrate in history the memorial of its Lord: herein lies the root of the mandate which he has entrusted to it. Now, the biblical memorial is not a simple remembrance of a past event, comparable to the western concept of memory, which connotes a movement from the present to the past through history as an expansion of the mind. The Hebrew terms *zikkaron*, *azkarah*, which the Greek translates as *anamnesis*, *mnemosunon*, indicate exactly the opposite movement. They express the act of making present a past event through an act of divine power:[4] that which has already taken place is re-presented, is made contemporary to the celebrating community.

This action of divine power is made clear by the totality of New Testament revelation as a bursting forth of the Holy Spirit, who realizes in history the paschal mystery of Christ, in which the whole Gospel is summed up. In this way the memorial is present as the event that most perfectly fulfills the evangelizing mission of the Church. In celebrating the memorial of the Lord, the Church becomes open to the action of the Holy Spirit, who makes present in different times and places the event of salvation, the object of the good news. Therefore if to evangelize means to obey the command of the Lord: "Do this in memory of me," and if the agent and the goal of the memorial is Christ himself in his Spirit, then evangelization has a typically christological and pneumatological character. It is the Spirit of Christ who evangelizes, because he makes the Christ of the Gospel present here and now.

The Church in turn must let itself be shaped by this outpouring of the Spirit, ardently invoking him as the one who brings the memorial of the Lord to fulfillment. Only in this way will evangelization be, not empty words of the flesh, but the power of God for the salvation of those who believe (cf Rom 1:16). And the Spirit, invoked by the Church, will make present that Christ who, himself anointed by the Spirit during his earthly existence (cf Mt 3:17; 4:1; Lk 4:14, 18, 21, etc.), has in turn sent the Spirit forth (cf Jn 20:22, etc.).

To Evangelize Means to Live in Communion with Christ and the Church

Openness to the Spirit, which the celebration of the memorial requires, must be shown in concrete actions and in a certain attitude of life that reproduces in our time the attitude of Christ celebrating his paschal mystery. In other words, in order that the Spirit may make Christ present and may enliven the Church, it is necessary that the community of believers prepare themselves for the celebration of the memorial by reliving the actions and choices of the Lord at the Last Supper.

How does Jesus present himself in the institution of the Eucharist? First of all he feasts with his followers. This fact creates between him and those who celebrate with him a profound bond of fellowship. In Israel the communion of those who feast together is a communion of life. A meal eaten together, especially on a solemn and special occasion, unites persons in a community so sacred that to violate it constitutes one of the most serious faults.[5] In an even more special way, the breaking of bread, with the distribution of a small piece to each person, and the sharing in the same cup of wine, are a sign of a profound solidarity in the sharing of a destiny.[6] Jesus thus explicitly unites the institution of the Eucharist to the banquet of fellowship. He does not choose as a sign of his gift just any bread and wine, in their basic materiality, but the bread and cup of fraternal love.[7]

The paschal memorial is ecclesial in its very sign and means. It follows, then, that the celebration of the Lord's memorial requires and establishes, for those who participate in it, communion in Christ and with one another. Without this communion, one does not celebrate this memorial in life and consequently does not evangelize. It is in the witness of sharing of life, of effective solidarity, that the Church becomes the center for the outpouring of the Spirit, to make present in time the Gospel of the Risen Savior.

This communion always has a universal and

local dimension. Insofar as the memorial makes the paschal mystery present in a particular place and time, its celebration implies fidelity to this concrete "here and now." In this way the Incarnation is prolonged analogically in the history of humankind, assuming different languages and cultures. At the same time, however, it is the one Christ "who suffered and is glorified" who in the Spirit is made present in a variety of times and places. This reality creates and calls for the catholicity (universality) of every act of evangelization, that is, the presence in it of the entire Christian mystery and the necessary openness to the communion of all the churches. Evangelization must be catholic in the twofold sense of this term: it must make present the whole Christ (*katholou* means in fullness) for the whole person, for all peoples, to the farthest boundaries of the world (*katholikos* means universal). One does not evangelize unless one is in communion with the whole Church, announcing the whole Gospel to the whole person and—at least in intention—to every person.

To Evangelize Means to Share in the Destiny of the Suffering Servant

The communion which the memorial establishes between the participants and Christ demands their participation in his destiny. The Old

Testament references in the accounts of the institution agree in delineating this destiny as that of the Servant. In fact, the Songs of the Suffering Servant of Yahweh from Deutero-Isaiah, let one glimpse the conclusion of a covenant (cf Is 42:6; 49:8), a new one (42:9), which will be fulfilled in the person of the Servant (42:6; 49:8). While they evoke the sacrificial image of the lamb (cf 53:7), they teach the expiation of sins through the substitution of an innocent victim (53:10-12), containing the "*peri (uper) pollon*," ("for many") which figures in Matthew 26:28 and Mark 14:24.[8] The influence of the Old Testament figure of the Servant on the scene of the Last Supper is thus evident. It is, moreover, confirmed by the evangelist Luke, who in the context of the Supper refers to two sayings about the service of those in authority (Lk 22:24-27), and by John, who sees in the episode of the washing of the feet the perfect expression of the interior meaning of the eucharistic institution, about which he does not speak.[9] The bond between the Servant of Yahweh and the Supper is therefore not accidental, but is part of the very meaning of the eucharistic banquet.

In virtue of the fraternal bonds uniting the participants, the eucharistic community must share in the destiny of the Servant, becoming a servant itself. In partaking of the Body given, through the strength it receives, it must become the ecclesial Body given, the Body for others, the

Body offered for the multitudes. In the paschal memorial the Church is born as a servant-people, a community of service.

From this stem important consequences for the Church's evangelizing mission. To evangelize, as to celebrate in life the memorial of the Lord, is a service, and it therefore requires "servants." Here is found the need for valuing the various ministries and charisms that the Spirit raises up, and thus for viewing the ordained ministry within a Church which is ministerial in its entirety.[10] The common participation of the baptized in the destiny of the Servant evidences the coresponsibility of all the faithful in the work of evangelization. In addition, the character of "service" brings to a resolution within the evangelizing mission the ecclesial dilemma about "identity-relevance."[11] In evangelizing, the Church not only affirms its own identity, but also renders the most fruitful service to the world. On the other hand, in serving humakind and working for human promotion, the Church does not lose its own identity, which is that of a servant-people, sharing in the destiny of the servant Christ.

Finally, solidarity with the Suffering Servant of the Lord sheds light on another aspect of the task of evangelization, which we shall call the mission beneath the cross. In other words, if Jesus in the memorial offers himself as the One who suffers out of love, the Church, in celebrating its

Lord's memorial in history, knows that it must share in the mystery of suffering. Evangelization is not the work of triumphalism or of colonial conquests. The Gospel is made present wherever the people of God completes in its flesh the passion of the Son of Man. In the poverty of suffering, in the lack of human means, in the trial of persecution, in the discreet and faithful presence of an apparently fruitless love, Christians celebrate in their lives the memorial of the cross. In this way they make the Gospel of the suffering of God living and present: the Gospel of his love and of our salvation.

To Evangelize Means to Anticipate the Feast of the Kingdom

Finally, at the Last Supper Jesus presents the eschatological tension proper to his memorial. He announces that he will no longer drink of the fruit of the vine until the day when he will drink it anew with his followers in the Kingdom of his Father (cf Mt 26:29; Mk 14:25), that is, until the Kingdom comes (cf Lk 22:18). In eating the bread and drinking from the cup of the Eucharist, the faithful announce the death of the Lord until he comes (cf 1 Cor 11:26). The new paschal banquet thus recalls another banquet, the definitive one of the Kingdom, of which it is the foretaste and the promise, and toward which it makes the history of the world ascend.

The memorial that Jesus entrusts to his Church thus becomes the Eucharist of hope, of openness to the future promise of God. From this flows a twofold task for the Church's evangelizing mission. Above all, it must always be the announcement of the divine advent, and therefore a challenging force in the present, a critical awareness of human events. In bringing to every situation the strength of its eschatological promise, the ecclesial announcement cannot be separated from denunciation, nor can the appeal to the future be separated from the challenge of the present in everything that presents a hindrance to the renewing action of the Spirit.

In the second place, to celebrate in life the memorial of hope signifies for the Church a constant proclamation of its own temporary nature, in the knowledge of being the Kingdom in rudimentary form, of living in the "penultimate" days, the season "between spring and summer," between what was already fulfilled in the paschal mystery of Christ and what is yet to come in the parousia.

From this comes the duty of the believing community to live in a state of perpetual searching and purification. Faithful to the past, it is always looking toward the future, ceaselessly tending toward the fullness of divine truth, until in it the words of the Lord reach their fulfillment (cf *Dei Verbum*, 8). The evangelizing Church does not announce itself. By celebrating in history the memorial of the new Pasch, it points out the future goal, judges the present, and imbues people with the strength of hope. In this manner, it purifies itself, because it exposes its own misery to the salvific judgment of the Spirit, who in an ever new way bursts into the history of humankind and projects it toward the coming of God. Evangelization constantly reminds the Church of its poverty and at the same time of its hope.

Conclusion

The Last Supper thus presents to us in a vivid and meaningful way the passage from the Word of the Servant to the servants of the Word, from Christ the evangelizer to the Church as evangelizer. In the Eucharist evangelization appears as the celebration in history of the memorial of the Lord. It implies the presence and action of the Spirit, communion with Christ in the ecclesial communion, participation in the destiny of the suffering Servant, the anticipation of the promised coming. The characteristics conferred by Jesus upon the evangelizing mission of his Church are clearly distinguishable: they are the christological, pneumatological, ecclesial, diaconal and eschatological dimensions of evangelization. In other words, in the light of the Lord's Eucharist, to proclaim the Gospel to the farthest bounds of the world means: to re-present Christ in a diversity of times and places, in the power of the Spirit, in ecclesial communion, in service to the world and beneath the sign of the Cross, preparing the promised glory of the Kingdom.

Prayer of Thanksgiving and Petition

*That reflection on the Word may more easily become
the nourishing and joyous experience of the Mystery*

We give you thanks, Father,
for this memorial of our origins rooted in you,
the memorial of the holy Supper,
in which your Spirit,
the first Gift to believers,
comes to make present for us
the reconciling Passover of your Son.
We bless you,
because the one bread and the one cup
gather us into the one Body,
making of us,
in the union of the Holy One
and through his holy gifts,
the communion of saints
in time and for eternity.
We give you thanks,
Lord of heaven and earth,
because this banquet
anticipates the feast of your Kingdom,
and, while it sustains us poor pilgrims,

it makes us vigilant and active
in working in history for justice and peace,
filling our hearts with hope and joy.

We bless you, Lord Jesus Christ,
who willed to entrust to your Church
the memorial of your Passover.
Grant that our entire existence
may humbly remain under your word
    of mission:
"Do this in memory of me."
Enable us, therefore,
to celebrate in life and in history
the powerful memory of your passion
and of your resurrection,
through the gift of your Spirit,
who fulfills in time the holy promise.
Grant that, docile to him,
we may always know how to be transformed,
in such a way that your action of grace
    becomes ours,
your sacrifice ours,
and the yes which the Father pronounced
    over you
may also resound in our lives.
Grant also that,
united in the Spirit
by the mystery of your Body and your Blood,
we may know how to live in communion
and to grow in communion,

giving to our actions a breath of the Church
according to the mission you entrust to each
   one of us.

We bless you, Lord Holy Spirit,
you who are desire in the heart of the Church,
you who are the fulfillment of our prayer!
We give you thanks
because by sanctifying the gifts that we offer,
you make Christ present for us,
and you make of us his Body living in history.
May you be the first agent
of the evangelization of the Kingdom
in the deeds and in the days of our lives.
Enrich us with your gifts,
so that we may place them at the service
of the community of our brothers and sisters
for the growth of the whole human family.
Help us to carry the cross with love,
until the day of the dawn
of the Glory that is awaited and longed for.
In you, through Christ our Lord,
we shall go to the Father,
and the holy banquet
of this present day
will be for us the living and delightful pledge
of the banquet in which we shall eat
of the bread of the Kingdom.
Amen! Alleluia!

Notes

Chapter 1

1. K. Rahner, "Il Dio trino come fondamento originario e trascendente della storia della salvezza," in *Mysterium Salutis* 3, Brescia, 1969, 404.

2. I. Kant, *The Conflict of the Faculties.*

3. K. Rahner, "Il Dio trino...," *op. cit.*, 414. For the full text that follows, cf B. Forte, *Trinità come storia: saggio sul Dio cristiano,*" Rome, 1985, where the ideas outlined here are more amply expounded and documented. [Available in English as *The Trinity as History: Saga of the Christian God,* New York, Alba House, 1989.]

4. G. Baget-Bozzo, *La Trinità,* Florence, 1980, 1ff.

5. A. Milano, "Trinità," in *Dizionario Teologico Interdisciplinare* 3, Turin, 1977, 495.

6. Cf B. Forte, *La chiesa icona della Trinità: breve ecclesiologia,* Brescia, 1985 [available in English as *The Church: Icon of the Trinity,* Boston, St. Paul Books & Media, 1991], and E. Peterson, *Il monoteismo come problema politico,* Brescia, 1983, put into clear perspective in G. Ruggieri's editorial, "Resistenza e dogma," 5-26.

7. G. Baget-Bozzo, *La Trinità, op. cit.,* 237.

8. K. Gibran, *Il Profeta,* Milan, 30.

9. Cf W. Popkes, *Christus traditus: eine Untersuchung zum Begriff der Dahingabe in Neuen Testament,* Zurich, 1967.

10. Cf G. Rossé, *Il grido di Gesù in croce: una panoramica esegetica e teologica,* Rome, 1984.

11. In the intertestamental texts, banishment or exile is a time of absence of the Spirit, spent in expectancy of the messianic outpouring of the Spirit Himself: cf *Psalms of Solomon* 17:42; *Enoch the Ethiopian* 49:2; *Testament of Judah* 24:2; *Testament of Levi* 18:7. The paschal account shows a Messiah who enters into the exile of the absence of the Spirit to then refill this exile with the new outpouring of the gift of the Spirit.

12. International Theological Commission (CTI), "Some Matters regarding Christology," in *Civiltà Cattolica* 131 (1980) no. 3129, IV D.8.

13. J. Moltmann, *Trinità e Regno di Dio*, Brescia, 1983, 41.

14. H.U. von Balthasar, "Mysterium paschale," in *Mysterium Salutis* 6, Brescia, 1971, 258.

15. CTI, "Some Matters...," *op. cit.*, IV C. 3.5.

16. J. Moltmann, *Il Dio crocifisso*, Brescia, 1973, 287.

17. *Ibid.*, 288.

18. H. U. von Balthasar, "Mysterium paschale," *op. cit.*, 341ff.

19. Cf Acts 2:24; 3:15; 4:10; 5:30, etc., as well as 1 Thes 1:10; 1 Cor 6:14; 15:15; 2 Cor 4:14; Gal 1:1; Rom 4:24; 10:9; 1 Pt 1:21, etc.

20. Cf B. Forte, *Gesù di Nazaret, storia di Dio della storia*, Rome, 1984, 92ff.

21. H. U. von Balthasar, "Mysterium paschale," *op. cit.*, 346.

22. Cf J. Pieper, *Sull'amore*, Brescia, 1974, 30ff.

23. Cf DS 125.

24. Cf DS 150.

25. From the second half of the fifth century, of western origin: DS 75.

26. 11th Council of Toledo (675); DS 528.

27. Cf *Summa Theol.* I, q. 39, a. 2.

28. Cf *ibid.*, q. 29, a. 4.

29. Cf *De Trinitate* 15, 6, 10.

30. *Ibid.*, 8, 8, 12.

31. *Ibid.*, 8, 10, 14.

32. *Ibid.*, 6, 5, 7.

33. E. Jüngel, *Dio, mistero del mondo*, Brescia, 1982, 409.

34. *Ibid.*, 427.

35. *Ibid.*, 486.

36. Cf *ibid.*, 503.

37. *De Fide Orthodoxa*, I 14: *PG* 94, 860.

38. Cf St. Hilary of Poitiers, *De Trinitate*, 3, 4: *PL* 10:78a; St. Augustine, *De Trinitate* 6, 10, 12; St. Thomas, *Summa Theol.*, I, q. 42, a. 5; St. Bonaventure, *Sent.* I d. 19 p. q. 4; etc. Cf also the *Decretum pro Iacobitis* of the Council of Florence (1442): DS 1331.

39. Cf DS 1330 and St. Anselm, *De processione Spiritus Sancti* 2: *PL* 158, 288 C.

40. Cf, for instance, *Summa Theol.*, I, q. 39, a. 7.

41. Cf H.U. von Balthasar, "Fides Christi," in Id., *Sponsa Verbi*, Brescia, 1972, 41-72.

42. Cf the *Theses* of the "politically oriented" group prepared at the Congress of the Italian Theological Association of 1983 in *Rassegna di Teologia* 25 (1984) 88, *Thesis 1*.

43. A quotation from *The Iliad*, which Aristotle uses to close his 12th

Book of *Metaphysics* and which Peterson, *Il monoteismo... op. cit.*, places *in capite libri*: 31.

44. J. Moltmann, *Trinità e Regno di Dio, op. cit.*, 212.

45. *Thesis 2, cit.*

46. *Thesis 4, cit.*

47. *Thesis 3, cit.*

48. *Thesis 5, cit. Thesis 6* is an invitation to discern the signs of the Spirit in the Word and in history, especially through the contribution of trinitarian theology.

49. Cf B. de Margerie, *La Trinité chrétienne dans l'histoire*, Paris, 1975, 367ff, as well as the comments of St. Augustine on the family as the image of the Trinity: *De Trinitate*, 12, 5, 5.

Chapter 2

1. 11th Council of Toledo: DS 528.

2. F. Rosenzweig, *La stella della redenzione*, Casale Monferrato, 1985, 167 and 176.

3. G. Marcel, *Homo viator*, Paris 1944, 189.

4. G. W. F. Hegel, *Lessons on the Philosophy of Religion*. For an interesting philosophical-theological reflection on love, cf J. Pieper, *Sull'amore*, Brescia, 1974 (a classic), then A. Nygren, *Eros und Agape*, 2 vols., Gutersloh, 1937.

5. *Il Profeta*, Milan, 1983, 30.

6. Cf B. Forte, *Trinità come storia: saggio sul Dio cristiano*, Milan, 1985, especially parts I and IV.

7. Cf *ibid.*, parts II and III, and also E. Jüngel, *Dio mistero del mondo*, Brescia, 1982, especially 390ff.

8. St. Augustine, *De Trinitate*, 8, 8, 12.

9. *Ibid.*, 8, 10, 14.

10. *Ibid.*, 6, 5, 7.

11. E. Jüngel, *Dio, mistero del mondo, op. cit.*, 409.

12. F. Rosenzweig, *La Stella della redenzione, op. cit.*, 231.

13. Cf M. Nédoncelle, *La reciprocité des consciences*, Paris, 1943.

14. St. Augustine, *De Catechizandis rudibus*, 4, 7.

Part 2—Introduction

1. St. Augustine, *Sermon 272: PL 38*, 1247.

2. St. Cyprian, *De Oratione Dominica 23: PL 4*, 553.

3. *Lumen Gentium*, n. 3; cf the entire first chapter.

4. Cf the beautiful text of the Commission on Faith and Constitution

of the Ecumenical Council of Churches: *Baptism, Eucharist, Ministry.*
Turin, 1982, 27ff.

5. Given at the Twenty-fourth Liturgical-Pastoral Convention (Rome,
February 10-12, 1982) and at an encounter of missionary workers.

6. Naples, D'Auria, 1975.

Chapter 3

1. cf *Lumen Gentium*, ch. 1.

2. *Lumen Gentium*, n. 3.

3. *Preparatory Document, Congress of Lourdes*, ch. 1.

4. *Lumen Gentium*, n. 7.

5. *Lumen Gentium*, n. 8.

6. *Lumen Gentium*, n. 4.

7. St. Cyprian, *De Oratione Dominica, op. cit.*, 553.

8. Cf *Lumen Gentium*, nn. 10-12.

9. *Preparatory Document, Congress of Lourdes*, ch. 1.

Chapter 4

1. The problem of the context of the Last Supper has been much
debated, especially because of the chronology given by John, which
places the death of Jesus on the fourteenth day of the month of Nisan,
the passover vigil. He therefore seems to exclude the possibility that
the Supper was a passover banquet, celebrated on the night of that
vigil (cf Ex 12:5-6). The synoptic tradition affirms instead that Jesus ate
the Passover (cf, for example, Lk 22:15). Among the various attempts
at solving this contrast, important precisely for showing the paschal
character of the Supper and therefore the Lord's will to institute the
memorial of the new covenant, we recall that of A. Jaubert, *Le date de
la Céne: calendrier biblique et liturgie chrétienne*, Paris, 1957. According to
this author, Jesus followed the ancient Essene-priestly calendar, which
placed the Passover on Wednesday, thus setting the day of his death
on the fourteenth of Nisan of the official Jewish calendar. Also the
explanation offered by J. Jeremias, *Le parole dell'Ultima Cena*, Brescia,
1973, 97ff, according to whom John would have transformed in his
chronology the typology of the lamb immolated on the vigil.

2. On this cf J. Coppens, "L'Eucharistie, Sacrement et sacrifice de la
nouvelle Alliance: fondement de l'Eglise," in *Aux origines de l'Eglise*,
ed. by J. Giblet, Paris, 1965, 125-128.

3. In the light of the principles set forth in the volume *La chiesa
nell'Eucaristia: per un'ecclesiologia eucaristica alla luce del Vaticano II*,
Naples, 1975, I deepened from an ecclesiological-eucharistic viewpoint

various aspects of Christian reality: the theme of the laity, dealt with in the article of the same name in the *Dizionario Teologico Interdisciplinare*, Turin, 1977; the theme of the primacy and of the universal communion of the churches, in *Asprenas* 23 (1976); and now, in this work the theme of evangelization.

4. On the concept of memorial, cf, for example, the studies of F.J. Leinhardt, *Le sacrement de la sainte céne*, Neuchätel-Paris, 1948, 9-48; and M. Thurian, *L'Eucaristia Memoriale del Signore: sacrificio di azione di grazia e di intercessione*, Rome, 1967.

5. Cf J. Jeremias, *Le parole dell'Ultima Cena, op. cit.*, 253ff.

6. Cf, for example, H. L. Strack, P. Billerbeck, *Kommentar zum Neuen Testament aus Talmud und Midrasch*, II Band, Munich, 1924, 619-620.

7. On this, cf J.M.R. Tillard, *Eucaristia e fraternità*, Milan 1969.

8. Cf J. Coppens, *L'Eucharistie, op. cit.*, 152.

9. C. H. Dodd, *The Interpretation of the Fourth Gospel*, Cambridge, 1960, 393: "The passage 13:1-30 corresponds to the synoptic account of the Last Supper."

10. Cf *Tous responsable dans L'Eglise? Le ministére prebytéral dans L'Eglise tout entière "ministerielle,"* Assemblee plénière de l'Episcopat français—Lourdes, 1973; Paris, 1973.

11. In this regard, cf J. Moltmann, *Il Dio crocifisso*, Brescia, 1973, 15-41.

══ St. Paul Book & Media Centers ══

ALASKA
750 West 5th Ave., Anchorage, AK 99501 907-272-8183.

CALIFORNIA
3908 Sepulveda Blvd., Culver City, CA 90230 310-397-8676.
1570 Fifth Ave. (at Cedar Street), San Diego, CA 92101 619-232-1442;
  619-232-1443.
46 Geary Street, San Francisco, CA 94108 415-781-5180.

FLORIDA
145 S.W. 107th Ave., Miami, FL 33174 305-559-6715; 305-559-6716.

HAWAII
1143 Bishop Street, Honolulu, HI 96813 808-521-2731.

ILLINOIS
172 North Michigan Ave., Chicago, IL 60601 312-346-4228; 312-346-3240.

LOUISIANA
4403 Veterans Memorial Blvd., Metairie, LA 70006 504-887-7631;
  504-887-0113.

MASSACHUSETTS
50 St. Paul's Ave., Jamaica Plain, Boston, MA 02130 617-522-8911.
Rte. 1, 885 Providence Hwy., Dedham, MA 02026 617-326-5385.

MISSOURI
9804 Watson Rd., St. Louis, MO 63126 314-965-3512; 314-965-3571.

NEW JERSEY
561 U.S. Route 1, Wick Plaza, Edison, NJ 08817 908-572-1200.

NEW YORK
150 East 52nd Street, New York, NY 10022 212-754-1110.
78 Fort Place, Staten Island, NY 10301 718-447-5071; 718-447-5086.

OHIO
2105 Ontario Street (at Prospect Ave.), Cleveland, OH 44115 216-621-9427.

PENNSYLVANIA
214 W. DeKalb Pike, King of Prussia, PA 19406 215-337-1882; 215-337-2077.

SOUTH CAROLINA
243 King Street, Charleston, SC 29401 803-577-0175.

TEXAS
114 Main Plaza, San Antonio, TX 78205 210-224-8101.

VIRGINIA
1025 King Street, Alexandria, VA 22314 703-549-3806.

CANADA
3022 Dufferin Street, Toronto, Ontario, Canada M6B 3T5 416-781-9131.